MAKE MONEY TEACHING CROCHET

Launch Your Business,

Increase Your Side Income,

Reach More Students

Marie Segares

Host, Creative Yarn Entrepreneur Show

Make Money Teaching Crochet: Launch Your Business, Increase Your Side Income, Reach More Students by Marie Segares

Copyright © 2016 by Creative Yarn Entrepreneur, LLC. All rights reserved.

No part of this book may be reproduced, stored in a retrieval system, or transmitted in any form or by any means—written, electronic, mechanical, recorded, photocopied, or otherwise—without the prior written permission of the author, Marie Segares, or the publisher, Creative Yarn Entrepreneur, LLC.

Although the author and publisher have made every effort to ensure that the information in this book was correct at the time of publication, the author and publisher do not assume and hereby disclaim any liability to any party for any loss, damage, or disruption caused by errors or omissions, whether such errors or omissions result from negligence, accident, or any other cause.

Published by Creative Yarn Entrepreneur, LLC, New York, New York

Ordering information:

Books may be purchased in quantity by contacting the publisher, Creative Yarn Entrepreneur, LLC, by mail (Planetarium Station, P.O. Box 340, New York, NY 10024) or by email (marie@creativeyarnentrepreneur.com).

ISBN: 978-0-9906834-0-7 (epub/mobi ebook)

ISBN: 978-0-9906834-1-4 (print workbook)

10 9 8 7 6 5 4 3 2 1

1. Business & Economics/Home-Based Businesses

2. Crafts & Hobbies/Needlework/Crocheting

3. Art/Business Aspects

Editor: Regina H. Paul

Yarn Illustration: OpenClipartVectors via Pixabay

First Edition

To my grandmother, who taught me to crochet,

and to Matthew, who has always supported and encouraged my creative business endeavors.

CONTENTS

About This Book	i
Section 1: Getting Started	1
Section 2: The Business Side of Things	27
Section 3: Marketing (It's Not a Dirty Word)	53
Section 4: Prepping for Class	69
Section 5: Resources	81
Appendices	99
If You Enjoyed This Book	107

ABOUT THIS BOOK

MY STORY

I learned to crochet from my maternal grandmother in 1984 and have crocheted–off and on–ever since. In 2002, I picked up *Good Housekeeping: The Illustrated Book of Needlecrafts* and taught myself to read patterns. The possibilities of crochet opened up to me in a completely new way, and I fell in love with the craft. In 2007, I was working full time and finishing up graduate school. On a whim, I decided to enroll in the Craft Yarn Council's Certified Instructors Program in crochet at the Fashion Institute of Technology. I thought it would be a fun way to spend some time away from hefty readings and homework assignments while hanging out with other crochet lovers. I met some wonderful people, finally learned what an afghan hook is used for, and was introduced to broomstick lace for the first time.

Right after I finished the course, my grandmother was diagnosed with pancreatic cancer. She died soon afterwards. I found that crocheting was one way I could keep her memory alive while also doing something I loved, and I decided to put that CYC certification to use.

I started teaching part-time in 2008. Since then, I have taught hundreds of beginner students how to crochet and have helped even more students expand their skills. As a teacher, I've earned a steady side income, traveled to fiber festivals, and launched a career in the yarn industry that now includes designing as a freelancer, self-publishing, and more. I've also met some wonderful students, who are now friends.

In this book, I'm going to share what I've learned about starting a successful crochet teaching business. Whether you are new to teaching crochet or are hoping to grow your clientele, I look forward to taking this journey with you.

ABOUT THIS BOOK

This book is designed as a practical guide to start a crochet teaching business.

But...

Most crochet teachers do not make a full-time living from teaching alone. For some, teaching is the foundation of a side income to support their "crochet habit." For others, it's an enjoyable part-time experience to supplement their income from a full-time job. And, for those who are making a living full time in the yarn industry, it's one of several diverse income streams they might rely on.

There is useful information in this book for crocheters who are considering teaching as a hobby, and most of the information is transferable to teaching knitting (or other crafts) for profit. The focus, however, is on developing a sustainable part-time business teaching crochet.

HOW THIS BOOK IS ORGANIZED

This is a practical, hands-on guide designed to get you ready to start teaching or to expand your teaching business so you can make more money.

Section 1: Getting Started is all about you. You'll walk through a series of activities to refine your idea for a crochet teaching business—for today, for next year, and for the next five years.

Section 2: The Business Side of Things is focused on getting your business structure in place. If you have an established business, you might want to skim this section; however, if you are launching a business for the first time, a thorough read will be helpful.

Section 3: Marketing (It's Not a Dirty Word) is all about telling (and showing) both students and teaching venues about yourself and your talents so you can grow your business. Many crafters negatively associate marketing with sleazy, high-pressure sales tactics. Instead, you should think of marketing as an ethical way to share your enthusiasm and passion for crochet with people in order to bring this exciting hobby into their lives!

Section 4: Prepping for Class guides you through the process of getting ready to teach, including developing course descriptions, lesson plans, and more.

Section 5: Resources includes free and low-cost resources that can help you and your crochet business thrive.

Sample forms and templates can be found in the **Appendices**.

> CRO-PRO TIP: Throughout the book, you'll also find boxed Cro-Pro Tips with additional tactics and strategies I've picked up over the years.

Are you ready? Let's get started.

SECTION 1: GETTING STARTED

Before I start any new business venture, I find it helpful to ask myself a few questions. You might recognize these journalistic questions from elementary school: who, what, where, when, why, and how. Once I have a clear idea of my intentions and goals, I can align my plans with my goals.

This section will walk you through these questions and help you to think about the first steps for your crochet teaching business as well as your short-term and long-term plans.

Even if your business has already launched, this section will help you make sure that you are aligning your actions and plans with your short- and long-term goals.

WHY DO YOU WANT TO TEACH?

Let's start with **why**.

Why do you want to teach crochet?

There are many reasons you might be considering teaching crochet. Here are some common ones:

- *Bring in side income to supplement full-time work in another industry.* You might find that your full-time job doesn't allow you the financial flexibility you'd like or that you'd like to save more. Teaching crochet can create a great part-time income to help pay for household expenses or to allow you to "splurge."
- *Share your passion for the craft.* You might be one of many who have found that crochet has enriched your life, gotten you through a difficult time, or inspired your creativity. Your primary goal in teaching is to promote crochet, and you view your income from teaching as a way to cover your expenses.
- *Promote your book, pattern designs, or other elements of your existing crochet business.* For some teachers, time in the classroom is part of marketing other products, like crochet books, patterns, kits, yarn, and more.
- *Earn your primary income from teaching crochet.* Perhaps you want crochet teaching to be your primary source of income. Many crochet business owners find that teaching locally can provide steady cash flow for their crochet business. This can help when income from other elements of your business, such as freelance design, self-publishing, or blogging, fluctuate.
- *Supplement your income from your full-time crochet business.* On the other hand, if your full-time crochet business is based largely on other activities, you might think of teaching as a small piece of the larger puzzle that forms your total business income.
- *Or maybe it's just this: People keep asking you to do it!* Some crocheters find that their work inspires others to want to learn to crochet. Maybe you have finally decided to transform those requests from friends, family, coworkers, and acquaintances to teach crochet into tangible income.

Understanding your primary purpose for teaching will help you to focus your crochet teaching business. As a new crochet teacher, it is easy to find yourself pulled in many directions. By prioritizing your immediate, short-term, and long-term goals, you can focus your energies in the most valuable direction.

TAKE SOME TIME TO THINK ABOUT WHY YOU WANT TO TEACH:

Why do you want to teach crochet now? _____
_____
_____
_____
_____

Do you think teaching will represent the same thing to your business in one year? _____
_____
_____
_____
_____

How about in five years? _____
_____
_____
_____
_____

Keep the answers to these questions in mind as we move on to the next W–**who** are the students you want to teach.

WHO ARE THE STUDENTS YOU WANT TO TEACH?

Thinking about your target audience is critical for any business. Having an understanding of **who** your target audience is will allow you to tailor your classes, course descriptions, pricing, and promotions to the particular needs of your ideal students.

Some teachers are generalists. These teachers do not have a specific audience and are equally comfortable teaching adults and children, men and women, professionals and stay-at-home moms. Others feel they have to be generalists because there are limited resources for learning crochet in their local communities.

However, most teachers have personal preferences, personality traits, life experience, and technical and soft skills that cause them to focus on a specific niche audience.

You might choose your niche audience based on age, gender, professional status, cultural group, or health status.

AGE

- *Children.* Teachers who specialize in working with children generally have high energy and an understanding of child development (especially as it relates to motor skill development, attention, and basic reading and math skills). Children's crochet teachers may further focus on particular age groups, such as teenagers or elementary school children, or on children with specific social, mental, and/or physical challenges. When teaching children, remember that they don't have control over their finances and schedules. As a result, you'll need to focus your marketing on the adults in their lives, while focusing your instruction on your students' needs and interests.

- *Multi-age groups.* Some teachers emphasize family activities through classes that engage both parents and children. Teaching these courses requires all the skills necessary for teaching both children and adults separately, along with the ability to bring the two groups together into a well-organized class—remembering, for example, that children can get bored during classes that might seem too short to an adult. If you are teaching multi-age groups, consider requiring each child to be accompanied by an adult, establishing a minimum age for the children, and monitoring the discussion of the adult students to avoid off-color language and inappropriate topics.

- *Adults.* If you choose to focus on adults, you will need to think about teaching differently than your favorite grade school teacher did. Most adults take crochet courses voluntarily and expect teachers to cater to their learning needs and preferences. It is not uncommon for adult students to take breaks, arrive late or leave early, want to chat with their friends, and/or refuse to do "homework" (or out-of class practice). As a result, teaching adults requires more diplomacy than teaching children does.
- *Older adults/seniors/retirees.* With all the research about the health benefits of crochet and knitting—especially the relationship between these crafts and the reduced risk of Alzheimer's disease and dementia—there is a renewed interest in crochet among older adults. Teachers who work with older adults will need to be comfortable working with students who might have physical and memory challenges. Don't forget to bring along a hefty dose of patience and be comfortable with repetition. A sense of diplomacy is also helpful, especially if you are a younger teacher. Showing respect and deference to your students is very important when working with older adults.

GENDER

Many crochet and knitting teachers, for obvious reasons, focus on women as students. If you think you would work well with men as students, you could specialize in classes for men—an interesting niche market.

PROFESSIONAL STATUS

Some subgroups of adults have particular needs, interests, and preferences that a teacher would need to consider:

- *Professionals/working people.* People working in high-stress jobs may seek relaxation or companionship, for example, from crafting. This audience typically has an inflexible schedule, so evening classes after work, lunchtime classes (in a large workplace or office building), and weekend courses might be best.
- *College students.* Campus residential life staff are always looking for fun activities that promote engagement and healthy behaviors on campus, and college students might be interested in crochet for stress-relief, for creating bonds with other students, or for community service or

charity initiatives. College students generally prefer on-trend projects made in affordable and easily accessible yarns.

- *Stay-at-home parents.* Many stay-at-home parents are looking for activities that provide a break from child rearing and allow them to socialize with other adults. Crochet groups can be the perfect solution.

OTHER POSSIBILITIES

If you speak another language fluently or are very familiar with the craft traditions of a specific ethnic group, you might want to consider focusing on students from a specific **cultural background**.

Some teachers specialize in working with students with **health challenges**, such as individuals with developmental delays or individuals in recovery from brain injuries. As with children, you might need to market your classes to a different audience from your students, such as administrators in residential facilities, hospitals, or adult day-care programs.

Your local community could also offer other niche audiences. Each of these audiences will have slightly— or widely!—different preferences and interests. They also have different amounts of disposable income, but don't let that be your only consideration in choosing an ideal student. For example, many senior centers have a budget to pay for recreation teachers, thus enabling you to teach low-income older adults if that is your ideal audience.

> CRO-PRO TIP: If you live in an area with a lot of tourism, don't forget to consider visitors as potential students! Over the years, I've taught many one-session private lessons to people who were visiting New York City for work or with family and who needed some relaxing time to themselves.

TAKE SOME TIME TO THINK ABOUT WHO THE STUDENTS ARE THAT YOU WANT TO TEACH:

What type of crochet students do you most understand now? _____
_____
_____
_____
_____

What type of crochet students are you most excited about working with now? _____
_____
_____
_____
_____

With further training or experience, is there another type of student you would like to be teaching in one year? _____
_____
_____
_____
_____

How about in five years? _____
_____
_____
_____
_____

Keep the answers to these questions in mind as we move on to the next W-**what** you want to teach.

WHAT DO YOU WANT TO TEACH?

So **what** exactly do you plan to teach? Just as you could specialize in a target audience, some crochet teachers choose to specialize in the **content of their courses**.

There are several approaches to content specialization:

- *Some teachers teach only at one level*, such as beginner, intermediate, or advanced crocheters. Teachers who like to introduce new students to crochet may prefer teaching beginner courses. These teachers love seeing a newbie finally perfect a foundational skill. Beginner-focused teachers don't mind repetition and are likely to be more encouraging than challenging. Some teachers enjoy taking people "beyond the beginner" into the next level of crochet exploration. These teachers may want to challenge intermediate students to get outside of their comfort zones. And finally, some teachers really want to focus on the most advanced students. These teachers may want to teach design or train-the-trainer courses. On the other hand, some teachers are comfortable teaching at various skill levels and enjoy being able to offer a diversity of classes, separately targeting beginner, intermediate, or advanced crocheters.
- **Some teachers focus on specific crochet techniques**, such as hairpin lace, freeform crochet, or Tunisian crochet. In every craft, there are cycles of popularity. If you enjoy teaching a currently popular technique, your classes could be in higher demand. On the other hand, perhaps your passion for a particular technique is so strong that you have no interest in the latest trends. If you can convert prospective students to your way of thinking, your classes could still be packed!
- **Some teachers emphasize skill-building classes while others teach only project-based courses.** Understanding your preferences on the continuum from technique class to project class is critical. Some teachers prefer to allow students to choose their own projects, while focusing on specific skills; other teachers prefer to organize their courses around specific projects to be completed (which might or might not teach specific crochet techniques). Some teachers refine this project concept even further and teach classes focused only on certain types of projects, such as crocheted socks, shawls, or garments. Here, too, you might find that you prefer to generalize and offer many different crochet courses.

TAKE SOME TIME TO THINK ABOUT WHAT YOU WANT TO TEACH:

Based on your teaching goals and your ideal students, what type of content do you want to teach now?

_____
_____
_____
_____
_____

Is there something different you will want to focus your teaching business on in one year? _____

_____
_____
_____
_____

How about in five years? _____

_____
_____
_____
_____

Keep the answers to these questions in mind as we move on to the next W–**where** you want to teach.

WHERE DO YOU WANT TO TEACH?

There are as many different settings for teaching crochet as there are student audiences, so **where** would you like to teach?

Some of the most common crochet education settings are these:

- *Public libraries.* Generally speaking, library classes must be open to the public; therefore, you can't "pick and choose" your students. Your local library may have a budget for classes, or you may choose to volunteer your time to gain experience or to build a reputation.
- *Senior centers, adult day-care centers, and assisted-living facilities.* Crochet keeps people active and using both their motor skills and their minds. Crochet classes also make great social events. Many senior centers, naturally occurring retirement communities, and related spots welcome crochet teachers and have a budget to pay for recreational classes.
- *Yarn and crafts shops.* Some shops use staff to teach, and others bring teachers in so their employees can focus on other things. Chain stores generally require certification. You can learn more about certification in Section 5: Resources.
- *Community or recreation centers.* Many community centers offer creative classes for children and/or adults.
- *Continuing education programs.* Many colleges have expanded their continuing education offerings to include "wellness" or "personal enrichment" classes. Your local school district might also have a continuing education program or adult school.
- *Museums or galleries.* Museums or galleries with a textile focus are an especially good fit, but children's museums, folk art museums, and local history museums might also consider tailored crochet classes.
- *Your home.* Some people enjoy teaching in their home. Perhaps they didn't grow up in New York City in the mid-70s to early '90s like me. I'm just too paranoid to invite someone I don't know into my home. But if that doesn't worry you, remember to consider potential students' allergies if you smoke or have pets.
- *The student's home.* Some students feel comfortable inviting a teacher into their home. This can be a great option, especially for private lessons or private group lessons. If you are allergic to pets or smoke, you should ask about the home environment before agreeing to teach a class in a student's home.
- *An office, union, or professional organization.* Many companies are open to the idea of employees using their facilities after hours or during lunch for classes. Students might pay the

registration fee, while the employer provides space for free. Unions or other professional organizations may be willing to pay for classes for their members, assuming that certain enrollment requirements are met.

- *A coffee shop, bookstore, or food court.* Any conveniently located establishment that allows people to hang around for a few hours at minimal cost can be an ideal location for an individual private lesson.
- *Your local Crochet Guild of America (CGOA) chapter.* Many local chapters allow members to teach lessons during meetings or can arrange for lessons with discounts for members. It helps if you are teaching something unusual or more advanced. You can learn more about the CGOA in Section 5: Resources.
- *Schools, camps, and after-school programs.* If you plan to teach children, explore institutional options inasmuch as they could be easier to organize.
- *Public parks and atriums.* When the weather is mild, a public location (outdoors or indoors and unheated) can be a fun spot for a class.
- *Nonprofit and government organizations.* Organizations focusing on education, the arts, youth, seniors, or people with health challenges might be interested in organizing crochet classes on site for their clientele.
- *Hospitals and long-term care facilities.* If you are particularly interested in working with students with health challenges, consider developing a partnership with a local hospital, long-term care facility, or congregate living home.
- *Private (rented) classrooms.* Some teachers like to maximize control over their classroom environment and, thus, prefer to rent space and organize their own classes. Local co-working spaces, athletic clubs, nonprofit organizations, and schools often rent space at affordable rates.

In addition to these locations, there are local events where you might consider teaching:

- *Baby showers.* People often get crafty when babies are about to be born. How about a workshop on a pieced blanket that everyone can work on together?
- *Bachelorette parties.* Short projects, like garter belts and floral appliqués, are perfect for PG-rated bachelorette parties.
- *College and high school community service events.* Many schools are interested in service learning and community service projects. For many charity projects, the work can be divided up among many students of varying skill levels. Similarly, a charity that is the recipient

of donated handmade items (like a homeless shelter) might be interested in sponsoring off-site classes to increase their donations.
- 🧶 *Heath fairs and wellness events.* With so much documented support for the health benefits of crochet, this is another option to consider if you enjoy teaching "drop in" lessons.

Once you have more experience under your belt, you might want to consider conferences, festivals, and retreats. Some events are themed, and others are willing to consider many types of class proposals. Teaching at events can be a way to reach a wider audience while traveling.

In the best case, **the venues where you teach will be closely aligned with your target audience and the topics you would like to teach.** For example, you may find that local yarn shops and fiber festivals are more receptive to highly specialized content, such as Irish lace, while other venues will prefer beginner classes or drop-in/project-help courses. Individual private students meeting in the home will often prefer individualized course content.

As you consider different locations, realize that there are different benefits and challenges of teaching at specific venues. Here are some things to consider:

- 🧶 *Compensation and cost.* Some venues pay better than others, just as some venues cost more to rent or use than others.
- 🧶 *Services.* Some venues provide marketing, copying, food and/or beverages, and other services to you and your students.
- 🧶 *Privacy.* Some venues provide more privacy and quiet, while others are simply an open space.
- 🧶 *Facilities.* Some venues are more attractive, more accessible, safer, or more centrally located than others.

And, of course, virtual teaching is also an option if you are tech savvy. While some people really need a teacher at their side to help out with the mechanics, others can learn crochet easily from videos and pictures. You can create a multi-lesson video or photo-tutorial course series, or you can offer private 1:1 tutorials via Skype, Google Hangouts, or other private streaming services. You can find more information about video and online courses in Section 5: Resources.

TAKE SOME TIME TO THINK ABOUT WHERE YOU WANT TO TEACH:

Where do you want to teach crochet now? _____
_____
_____
_____
_____

Do you think you'll want to teach in the same location(s) in one year? _____
_____
_____
_____
_____

How about in five years? _____
_____
_____
_____
_____

Keep the answers to these questions in mind as we move on to the next W—when you want to teach.

WHEN DO YOU WANT TO TEACH?

When you teach will likely be constrained by your other commitments. If it isn't, decide whether you'd like to remain flexible or to specialize in daytime, afternoon, evening, or weekend classes. If teaching is going to be a substantial part of your full-time crochet business, you might need to be comfortable teaching at any time; but, in most other situations, your teaching time will be limited by the demands of the rest of your schedule.

Think about whether your availability a good fit with the ideal students–or target audience–you've identified. For example, if you want to teach professional women, evening or weekend hours would probably be ideal. If you are available only during the day, consider approaching large employers about offering lunchtime classes on site.

TAKE SOME TIME TO THINK ABOUT WHEN YOU WANT TO TEACH:

When can you teach crochet now?_____
_____
_____
_____

Do you think you'll want to teach at the same time(s) in one year? _____
_____
_____
_____

How about in five years? _____
_____
_____
_____

Keep the answers to these questions in mind as we move on to the final W (which is really an H)–how you want to teach.

HOW DO YOU WANT TO TEACH?

Let's talk about **how** you want to teach. Will your classes be "one-off" events (that is, a series of individual experiences), or do you plan to offer courses with multiple sessions? With the exception of fiber festivals and similar events, it is possible to specialize in either individual classes or multi-session courses in most other cases. And, of course, there are many teachers who offer both.

When I first started teaching, I organized many private group sessions. I would spend weeks developing a class, scouting low-cost (or free) locations, and then marketing the class. It soon felt as if I were on a hamster wheel. The cycle of recruitment for the next class would begin before the current class finished. I also found it difficult to jump back and forth between different topics. I learned that I really preferred multi-session courses, and I've actually specialized in teaching 4-week to 10-week classes in adult education settings. Although I occasionally offer a one-session event at a regional fiber festival or private lessons to individual students, I generally stick to the format that works for me. What do you think will work best for you?

TAKE SOME TIME TO THINK ABOUT HOW YOU WANT TO TEACH:

How do you want to teach crochet now? _____
_____
_____

Do you think you'll want to teach using the same structure in one year? _____
_____
_____

How about in five years? _____
_____
_____

Now, let's bring together all of your preferences before we explore the preparation you may need to get ready to teach!

BRINGING IT ALL TOGETHER

Now that you've thought through the 5 Ws (and that pesky H) for your crochet teaching, keep your preferences and plans in mind as you go through the rest of this book.

Be sure to keep your long-term goals in mind as you launch or refine your teaching business, or there's no way you'll reach them!

TEACHING GOALS

Use this worksheet to write down and track your teaching goals based on your answers to the journalistic (Who, What, When, Where, Why, How) questions and other plans you have for your teaching business.

Short-term goals (6 months - 1 year)	Medium-term goals (1 year - 4 years)	Long-term goals (5+ years)

ARE YOU READY TO START TEACHING?

To be a great crochet teacher, you'll need certain skills and qualities. Let's start with the essentials.

TECHNICAL SKILLS

As a teacher, you don't need to know everything, especially if you primarily teach beginners. However, a solid foundation in crochet is critical for your credibility and your confidence. You should also have a firm grasp of the standard names (and some common variants) of the major stitches and techniques.

Even if you don't have advanced skills, an understanding of the next level (beyond the basics) will make you a more versatile and confident teacher. Remember that, even in a beginner class, you will have some students who already have basic skills, and you will need to teach them, too.

If you're lacking in technical skills, don't worry! Section 5: Resources has some suggestions for how to develop your crochet skills further.

> CRO-PRO TIP: Use your learning experiences to improve your teaching! The frustrations and challenges you face while enhancing your technical skills are the same ones your students will have, and the strategies you use for overcoming them can be added to your teaching tool box.

SOFT SKILLS

In addition to technical skills in crochet, there are certain personal attributes and soft skills that will make you a stronger and more popular teacher, including these:

- *Communication Skills* - You will need to speak clearly and audibly, have several different ways to explain each technique or stitch, and be aware of your body language and nonverbal communication. In addition, you'll often need to use your powers of persuasion to market yourself and negotiate compensation.

- *Confidence* - You will need to project your voice, admit when you don't know something, resolve conflicts between students, deal with disruptive or monopolizing students, and negotiate rates and compensation. All of these social interactions require confidence. If you feel shaky about yourself and your skills, it will be obvious to your students and class coordinators.

- *Diplomacy* - This is especially critical when you're teaching adults. You will need to be able to redirect someone gently if she or he is making a mistake.

- *Energy* - When you're teaching, you will need to have a reasonably high level of energy. While you don't need the stamina of an aerobics instructor, you can't be dozing in the corner, either.

- *Organization and Time Management* - Structuring a class takes organization, whether it is for one student or a group. You will need to prepare your ideas and materials, meet your students on time (or, preferably, early), and have the right amount of content to cover. Depending on the situation, you may also need samples, handouts, or other materials. Careful pre-planning is required, especially in the beginning when you are developing course materials for the first time. You can find more planning tips in Section 4: Prepping for Class.

- *Patience* - If you don't like to repeat the same instructions multiple times, teaching crochet may not be for you. Or, at the very least, you may want to avoid teaching beginners! Remember that many of your beginner students have never tried crochet before. Others have had unsuccessful attempts to learn from a teacher, a book, a video, or an online resource. Your lack of patience could turn someone off forever from a great craft.

There is one other quality that is an absolute requirement for successful teaching: **passion for the craft**. It's rare to have a captive audience as a crochet teacher, so you must engage your students. Without enthusiasm and a love for the craft, it's very difficult to pull students in and retain them in your classes. Your passion and enthusiasm will also motivate students who are struggling. All of the other soft skills can be developed through practice and experience.

SOLIDIFYING YOUR SKILLS

Improving technical skills to an intermediate or advanced level should be a priority for a new crochet teacher. You can use Section 5: Resources to create a self-study course, or you can enroll in face-to-face or virtual classes to improve your own skills.

> CRO-PRO TIP: Observe the teacher (or author) as you're learning. You may want to adapt (or avoid) some of those teaching techniques.

What if you have strong technical skills, but your soft skills are not as well developed? Here are some ways to develop those so that you can be a better teacher.

PRESENTATION AND PUBLIC SPEAKING SKILLS

For many people, speaking in front of a group can be terrifying. (If this describes you, consider teaching individual lessons as you further develop your public speaking abilities.) Others don't feel nervous, but simply lack the skills to present clearly to a large audience. There are several key elements to consider —your voice, your eye contact and body language, and your content.

If public speaking is a challenge for you, consider taking a public speaking course through a local adult education program.

> CRO-PRO TIP: Whenever you take an adult education class, be sure to speak with the class coordinators about the possibility of offering a crochet class. Many adult education venues offer arts and crafts courses, creativity classes, or wellness/stress-relief classes, and crochet classes would definitely fit the bill.

Another way to improve your public speaking skills is by joining Toastmasters. (You can learn more about this organization in Section 5: Resources.) You can also record yourself using your webcam or smartphone camera as you rehearse your lesson. Review the recording and make adjustments, or ask a friend or family member for feedback.

PATIENCE

Sometimes, trying to see the situation from a different perspective can help develop patience. One of the major challenges I faced when I first taught crochet is that I didn't remember learning. My grandmother taught me to crochet when I was a child, and I felt as though I always knew how to crochet. Thinking about the experience and challenges of learning something new can help you develop patience. For example, you might try crocheting, knitting, or even writing with your nondominant hand. Since you're so skilled with your dominant hand, experiencing that frustration might help you empathize with your students and be more patient.

If a specific student triggers your impatience during class, consider moving around to another student. By taking a short break to help someone else, you can re-ground yourself.

Some teachers also find that meditation (or prayer) before class increases their tolerance for frustration and makes them more patient.

CONFIDENCE

One of the keys to teaching confidently is being prepared. When you know your content well, have multiple ways to present it, and have enough material to teach at a slow or fast pace, you will feel much more confident. Having detailed lesson plans, especially when you begin teaching, will allow you to rehearse and practice teaching. You can find more information in Section 4: Prepping for Class.

However, some of us struggle with confidence, even when we are very prepared and knowledgeable. One way to boost your confidence before you start "officially" teaching is to teach a friend or family member to crochet. Friends are a relatively low-risk group to teach because they can give you feedback gently if you ask for it—and, even if you "fail" to teach them, they will probably be understanding.

ORGANIZATIONAL SKILLS

Crochet teachers need to organize their time as well as their classroom materials and tools.

Keeping an annotated calendar of your teaching appointments helps you to structure your time. Some teachers prefer electronic methods, like the calendar available from a phone, tablet, or email program, while others (like me) prefer paper methods.

Start by setting an appointment for each class meeting, including the required travel time. Include a supply list for your class as well as contact information for the class coordinator and travel directions, if necessary. Set a reminder in your electronic system or by adding a note a few days in advance on your paper calendar.

You may find that students consider it rude when a teacher looks at a smartphone during class, so a watch or small digital clock to keep time during your session may be valuable. I always set an alarm for 15 minutes before the end of the session to review the class materials, answer questions from students, and make announcements about upcoming classes.

For multi-lesson classes, add notes about each session on your calendar. These might include student names, project or technique interests, or a list of supplementary materials to bring to the next session.

Organize your class materials by setting aside hooks, notions, at least two colors of yarn, paper, and pens in a bag or container. If you teach multiple courses, consider setting up separate containers with specific supplies, samples, and books for each course. This will save you time in the long run and ensure that you don't forget necessary materials.

Some teaching venues will provide a small cubby or drawer for crochet teachers. If you teach at such an organization, consider whether leaving materials on site would help you to be more organized about your class materials. You can read more about organizing class materials in Section 4: Prepping for Class.

ENERGY

There are many ways to increase your energy level when you teach. Start by getting a good night's rest and drinking plenty of water. You can become surprisingly dehydrated when you're teaching as you project your voice, walk around the room, and (potentially) deal with stressful situations. I find eating a small snack, like a banana or protein bar, before class helps.

Many teachers find that stretching, deep breathing, or meditation before class helps to improve their energy levels. (And don't forget to take a trip to the restroom before class starts.) When possible, you might also find it helpful to schedule classes during the time of day when you are naturally most energetic (e.g., before noon if you are a "morning person").

DIPLOMACY

I've found that understanding the different ways that people learn has helped me approach students more diplomatically. Research learning styles or people styles if you aim to be more diplomatic in your classroom interactions.

IS CERTIFICATION RIGHT FOR YOU?

Earning a crochet or teaching certification is one way to solidify your skills while also gaining a credential that could be useful for marketing purposes. The Craft Yarn Council (CYC) offers Certified Instructors Programs (CIP) in crochet. The CIP is available as a correspondence course or through periodic on-site trainings at colleges and fiber festivals.

> FULL DISCLOSURE ALERT! I'm a CYC certified crochet and knitting instructor (level I) and teacher (level II). I don't receive any compensation from the CYC for promoting the CIP. Personally, I consider both certifications money well spent, but your situation might make the training more or less valuable for you.

Here are several reasons you should consider a teaching certification:

- *Some employers require certification.* The certification programs were developed to help "big box stores," like Jo-Ann Fabric and Craft Stores and Michaels, recruit and retain skilled teachers. Certification is generally required in these settings.
- *Some organizations prefer certification.* While your local yarn shop, continuing education program, and regional fiber conference probably don't require you to be certified, having a credential may give you a boost over another interested teacher. This is particularly true if you don't have other credentials in the fiber arts, if you live in an area with a lot of competition, or if you have limited teaching experience.
- *You aren't confident about your teaching abilities.* The CIP on-site training focuses on how to teach the craft. (In my opinion, the correspondence course focuses primarily on technique and less on teaching the craft.) If you don't know how to provide step-by-step instructions or why a stitch should be formed in a certain way, the certification program can help you prepare to teach.
- *You need a head start on developing your teaching resources.* The CYC maintains a teacher's portal on its website, which includes materials you can adapt for use with your students. It also offer tips and materials for publicizing your Michaels classes.
- *It just sounds cool.* When I tell students about what I had to do to complete my certification, it often puts them at ease and makes them feel more comfortable about taking a class with me.

On the other hand, here are reasons you might decide against certification:

- 🧶 *It costs money.* Registration for the CIP is currently $170. Attending an on-site program can be very costly if you need to travel to the location.
- 🧶 *It takes time.* The on-site program is two and a half days long. The correspondence program can take months to complete. Both programs require you to teach for 15 to 30 hours to earn certification.
- 🧶 *It isn't necessary if you have sufficient experience or education in crochet already.*
- 🧶 *There isn't much competition in your local area, so the certification provides no advantage.* I live in New York City, and everyone and her mother wants to teach crocheting. But perhaps where you live, you are the only game in town.

An alternative to teaching certification is to become a Master of Advanced Crochet Stitches and Techniques through the Crochet Guild of America. While this program does not specifically prepare you to teach, it provides structure for advanced technical training as well as an assessment of your skills. This can also be helpful in providing you with a credential to help you improve credibility and marketability.

Now that you have an understanding of your teaching goals and the preparation and training you need, let's talk about how to formalize your crochet teaching business.

MARIE SEGARES

PROFESSIONAL DEVELOPMENT PLAN

Use this worksheet to create and track your professional development plan based on your self-assessment of skills you need to improve, feedback from student evaluations, and ideas from Section 5: Resources.

Short-term skills to improve (6 months - 1 year)	Medium-term skills to improve (1 year - 4 years)	Long-term skills to improve (5+ years)

SECTION 2: THE BUSINESS SIDE OF THINGS

SO, SHOULD YOU FORMALIZE YOUR BUSINESS?

Let me start by saying that I'm neither a lawyer nor an accountant. You may wish to consult with one (or both) of these professionals before launching any new business venture.

Many teachers do not formalize their teaching business by choosing a business entity and registering it locally, but there can be advantages to doing so. Here are just a few reasons why you might want to consider formalizing your business:

- It may be difficult to secure a business banking account without formalizing your business, and you may have a harder time accurately tracking your earnings and expenses inside of a personal banking account.
- If you teach from home, you may find that your renter's or homeowner's insurance doesn't cover incidents that arise from teaching. You may need a separate policy for home-based businesses.
- You may find it keeps your business costs lower by allowing you to buy products wholesale or at a substantial discount.
- You may be able to provide more protection for your personal assets in the event of legal action arising from your business activity.
- You may find that you are more accountable to your teaching goals once you formalize your business.
- Your customers and family may respond more positively to the formality of an established business entity. (In other words, people may take you–and your business–more seriously.)

There are some downsides, too, like these:

- It takes some time and effort to research the right business entity for you and your business and to figure out the logistics of applying within your locality.
- Once you make a choice, you'll have to pay fees, and you may have to enlist the support of a lawyer or an accountant (or both).

If you do decide to formalize your business, there are many different business types to consider. However, there are two types of business entities I have seen frequently among crochet teachers: sole proprietorship (sometimes called a DBA or "doing business as" certificate) or a limited liability company (often abbreviated as LLC).

Although each business entity type may vary slightly in your local area, generally speaking...

Sole proprietorships are owned by one person, who is often an owner-operator:

- As a sole proprietor, you will report your business income and expenses as part of your own personal income taxes.
- In most states, registering as a sole proprietor is the least expensive and easiest type of business entity to form, and it allows you to apply for a sales tax certificate (if your crochet business sells physical products or if your state taxes classes) and to operate your business under another name (your business name), without seeming like a shady criminal with an alias.
- Being a sole proprietor provides virtually no liability protection. In other words, if someone sues you, your personal assets, as well as your business's assets, could be at risk.

In most states, a **limited liability company** can be owned by one or more persons:

- The paperwork is generally more complex to set up (and the fees higher) than for a sole proprietorship.
- LLC owners have the option of reporting their income for tax purposes as individuals or as a corporation.
- This type of business, as the name suggests, provides more liability protection because it creates more separation between the business and the individual.

In addition to these two types of business entities, there are other options available. If you do decide to formalize your crochet business, you'll want to choose the best option for you. (By the way, you can always change your business entity type later—with additional fees and paperwork, of course.)

Start by looking through your local or state government's resources for starting a business. In the U.S., you can also find information and free resources through your local Small Business Administration District Office or Small Business Development Center or by meeting with a SCORE counselor. You may find that a conversation with a business counselor can help you make a more informed decision about your next steps. You can find more information about these options in Section 5: Resources.

SHOW ME THE MONEY

Whether your crochet teaching business is formal or informal, you'll need to make arrangements for getting paid. In this section, we'll discuss payment options; payment, refund, and cancellation policies; pricing; and sales and self-employment taxes.

PAYMENT OPTIONS

If you plan to make a business out of teaching crochet, you'll need to explore different payment options and choose the one (or more than one) that will work best for you and your business. Some options to consider are cash payments, checks, money orders, and in-person and online merchant payment systems.

CASH

If you teach private, face-to-face classes, you can opt to be paid entirely in cash.

Cash has advantages as a payment system:

- No vendor/merchant account fees will be deducted, so you keep more of your earnings than with many other payment options.
- Cash also provides an immediate cash infusion to your business, allowing you to pay bills, invest in your business, or pay yourself right away.

However, cash has disadvantages, too:

- It can easily be lost or stolen and can't be replaced.
- You'll need to implement your own system for tracking cash payments.
- Some teachers might find it harder to separate business income in cash from their personal or household finances.
- It is very difficult (or impossible) to arrange for prepayment. As a result, you might not be able to anticipate if group classes will fill or to enforce cancellation policies.
- Many venues discourage (or prohibit) teachers from accepting cash payments while on site.

If you decide to accept cash payments, I recommend setting up a system both for providing receipts and for tracking your income *before* your first payment is received. Consider accepting cash payments only from students or venues you have an established relationship with and requiring pre-payment using another payment option from other students and venues.

CHECKS, E-CHECKS, AND MONEY ORDERS

Many venues provide payment by check, e-check, or money order, and you may also agree to accept any of these as payment for private lessons.

These options have several advantages as a payment system:

- Many business clients pay only by check (or e-check) and have established procedures in place for recovering lost checks.
- Check, e-check, and money order payments are relatively easy to track as deposits into a business banking account.
- These payments allow you (or the class venue) to accept pre-payment or deposits for registration, ensuring that you will have enough students to make it financially worthwhile to teach a group class.

There are some downsides to these options as well:

- Personal checks can bounce, and your financial institution may charge you a fee as a result.
- Checks and money orders are physical objects and, therefore, need to be hand-delivered or mailed. As a result, registration deadlines will need to be well in advance of a class to allow for sufficient registration. You may lose out on last minute or impulse registrations as a result.

- 🧶 Many no- or low-fee small business accounts limit the number of transactions you may process in a given month. To save on bank fees, you may have to hold checks until you have several in order to make a batch deposit, which makes it unlikely that you'll see the full benefits of pre-payment.
- 🧶 Checks and money orders may take several days to clear, so you may experience a lag in cash flow. This may be especially pronounced over weekends or during holiday periods.

You may choose to accept only business checks and to require private students to pay by money order or another payment system in order to avoid some of the negative aspects of these payment methods.

IN-PERSON AND ONLINE MERCHANT PAYMENT SYSTEMS

In-person merchant payment systems (sometimes called "point-of-sale" or POS systems) are modern conveniences that could make working with private students smoother. These systems allow you to accept electronic payments at a venue through credit cards, ATM/bank cards, and more through the use of a tablet, smartphone, or laptop. Online systems allow students and venues to send you electronic payments in advance or after you complete a class series.

There are advantages to using merchant payment systems:

- 🧶 Tracking and financial reports are automated and frequently customizable.
- 🧶 Payments are instantaneous, providing may of the same benefits of cash, but can be completed in advance for pre-registration.

The main disadvantage is that the huge array of options available can be overwhelming. Each method also charges fees, which could mean that you need to raise your prices. Personally, I use PayPal for online payments, and I've used Square for in-person payments in the past. You can read more about these services and other merchant payment options in Section 5: Resources.

PAYMENT, REFUND, AND CANCELLATION POLICIES

Once you've decided how you can accept payments, it's time to think about payment, refund, and cancellation policies. If you plan to teach private lessons (in addition to or instead of classes organized through another venue), your policies will help your students understand what they are paying for and may also provide you with some legal protection in the event of a disagreement with a student.

In a perfect world, payments would be timely, no one would ever cancel a course, and you would never have to issue a refund. In the real world, you'll want to develop policies that can help protect you from "worse-case scenarios."

> CRO-PRO TIP: Before writing your own policies, review the "fine print" from your bank and merchant payment system so you understand fees, timelines, or other issues you might want to incorporate. Similarly, review the payment, refund, and cancellation policies of any venues where you teach. You'll have a better understanding of the impact of these policies on your students and your classes, and you might even find some language you'd like to adapt for your own policies.

PAYMENT POLICY

At a minimum, your payment policy should answer the following questions:

How does your business accept payment? _____
_____
_____
_____

MAKE MONEY TEACHING CROCHET

Does your business require pre-registration with full payment or with a deposit? If so, how far in advance do students need to pre-register? _____

_____
_____
_____
_____

Do you offer discounts to students who pre-register and/or pay with cash? _____

_____
_____
_____
_____

Do your course fees include sales tax? If not, will you be collecting additional taxes from the student?

_____
_____
_____
_____

Do your course fees include materials/supplies? If not, will students be responsible for bringing their own materials, or will you charge an additional fee for materials? _____

_____
_____
_____
_____

Does your business collect an additional charge for bounced checks or rejected payments (if applicable)? _____

_____
_____
_____
_____

As an example, your payment policy for private students might read like this:

Sally's Crochet School accepts money orders and credit/charge payments via PayPal. Students must pre-register with a 50% deposit at least 5 business days before the first day of class in order to reserve a spot. Students who pre-register with full payment at least 15 business days before the first day of class will receive a 10% discount. Course fees include the cost of materials.

Draft your payment policy here: _____
_____
_____
_____
_____
_____
_____
_____
_____
_____
_____
_____
_____
_____
_____
_____
_____
_____
_____
_____
_____
_____
_____

Refund and Cancellation Policies

Issues related to refunds often overlap with cancellations, so you should write these policies at the same time.

At a minimum, your refund policy should answer the following questions:

Will you provide a complete or partial refund to students who prepay, but are unable to attend classes? If so, how far in advance of the classes must they notify you? _____
_____
_____
_____
_____

If you provide only partial refunds, how are the amounts determined? _____
_____
_____
_____
_____

Will you offer a credit towards another course if you don't offer refunds? How long does the student have to redeem this credit? _____
_____
_____
_____
_____

Your cancellation policy should answer the following questions:

Will you cancel group classes with low enrollment? If so, how and when will students be notified? _____
_____
_____
_____
_____

How will you notify students if classes need to be cancelled due to weather or other external events, personal illness or family emergency, or facilities issues at the venue where you meet? _____
_____
_____
_____
_____

If classes are cancelled, will students receive a full or partial refund or credit? _____
_____
_____
_____
_____

As an example, your refund and cancellation policies might read like this:

Sally's Crochet School will notify students 3 days in advance of class cancellations due to low enrollment. Students who pre-registered with full or partial payment will receive a refund within 72 hours of cancellation.

In the event of an emergency, Sally's Crochet School will notify students about class cancellations using the phone number provided at the time of registration. Students will have the option of receiving a refund within 72 hours of cancellation or applying their course fee to a make-up class. Make-up classes must be taken within 12 months or students will forfeit their registration fee.

Draft your refund policy here:

Draft your cancellation policy here: _____

_____

_____

_____

_____

_____

_____

_____

_____

_____

_____

_____

_____

_____

_____

_____

_____

_____

_____

_____

_____

_____

I recommend writing your policies in common language and not in "legalese," unless you've actually consulted a lawyer during their development. This approach will humanize your business for your potential and existing students and reinforce for them that you aren't an impersonal, mega-business.

PRICING

Now that you've thought about how you will bring in and process payments for your classes, it's time to talk about pricing.

Before we start, let's just clear up the difference between "price" and "cost", since sometimes these words are mistakenly used interchangeably:

- The **price** is the amount of money you ask the student to pay for your class or for each hour of your class.
- The **cost** is how much your business spends on the class. This includes your own labor, travel and preparation time, and more.

> CRO-PRO TIP: Before you set your prices, do a little market research. Find out what local yarn shops, adult education venues, "big box" craft stores, and private teachers in your area are charging for crochet (or knitting or other related crafts) lessons. Most of this research can be done online by looking at a shop's or adult education venue's website or by searching local websites, like Craigslist. You may also want to make a few phone calls and act as a prospective student.

Entire books have been written on pricing strategies, but I'll focus on just a few that you might find useful.

COST-PLUS PRICING

If you have a very clear idea of how much it costs you to teach–including the time you take to prepare for the class, transportation to and from the venue, and your hourly rate–you may want to consider cost-plus pricing. In this approach, your price is your costs **plus** the amount of profit you'd like to make.

Cost-plus pricing can be a difficult approach for a service business (like teaching) since there are many factors that contribute to your costs. For example, it might be difficult at the beginning to determine what percentage of your total crochet business income will come from teaching, so you might struggle to allocate overhead costs, such as maintaining your website, post office box, or business cell phone service, across several income-producing activities.

INCOME TARGET PRICING

A related approach is to set an income target for your teaching. As an example, perhaps you'd like to earn $5,000 from teaching crochet in the coming year. In that case, you'd need to earn $125/week from teaching for 40 weeks. If you teach a weekly two-hour class, your rate will need to be $62.50/hour. (Side note: If you choose this approach, don't use 52 weeks for your calculations. Crochet lessons are really not a year-round activity. Even the most devoted, ongoing students need time off from lessons for major holidays, vacation, sickness, and so on.)

Setting an income target is a great goal-setting exercise, but the resulting price might not be feasible in your community for a variety of reasons or might be much lower than what other teachers are charging. I recommend doing this exercise anyway, so that you can determine how close the price of a particular class comes to moving you towards your income target for teaching.

DEMAND-MINUS PRICING OR GOING-RATE PRICING

If your community has a lot of options for prospective crochet students, you might find that prices have been driven down by relatively low demand for each teacher. In that case, you might need to choose the demand-minus approach, where you basically set your prices at what students are willing to pay and then lower your costs to make that price profitable for you. Perhaps you will not offer handouts, or perhaps students will not be able to choose custom-class options because you are unwilling to invest additional preparation time into a class where your hourly rate is low.

The benefit of this approach is that you won't be trying to compete on price (which often leads to lowering your price to a point where it is no longer worthwhile to teach), and you'll seem to be comparable to other options. That second part is also a potential disadvantage, since you'll have to work harder to explain to your prospective students why your classes are better or different from those taught by other teachers in the area.

As you might guess, if the prevailing rate for lessons in your area is very low, this is a very unfavorable approach to pricing—at least for teachers trying to earn money. It's great for students trying to save money!

In your local community, you might find that earning a relatively low rate teaching is still preferable to other options for side income, but I'd urge you to consider other pricing strategies before you assume this is your only choice.

PRESTIGE PRICING

We've all seen that some brands charge significantly higher prices for products that are quite comparable to products other companies are offering for lower prices. In this case, the brand is using prestige pricing. By setting a higher price, you send a signal to prospective students that your classes are "better" somehow than whatever else is available in the area, you increase your potential profit, and you have more flexibility for discounting.

If you choose a prestige pricing approach, you will set your prices higher than what is typical in your community, based on your market research. You will likely have a lower demand for your classes because some students will be unable to afford your rates; however, you'll be earning more for each hour you teach, so you might be able to teach less often and still earn the same amount of money.

If your prices are higher, you can also consider offering discounts. For example, you might offer students a 10% discount (or even a 25% discount, if your prices are high enough) for pre-registering with full payment, or you might offer a group discount on private lessons where you charge the same hourly rate for up to five students.

Prestige pricing is a great option if you already have a reputation as a designer, author, or teacher in the area. You must also project a lot of confidence, as you will probably get some push back on your prices. It helps to have a clear idea of why your classes are better than other options that are available for a lower price locally if you choose this approach.

BUNDLED PRICING

Another approach is to provide a bundled price for a combination of services and products. For example, you might charge one fee for a class that includes a supply kit, rather than separating the price of your teaching rate (a service) from the price of the supply kit (a tangible product). This might be a way to increase your prices without triggering push back from your students. This is also a helpful approach in venues that won't allow you to collect money for supplies from students while they are on site.

You can also use bundled pricing as a way to separate yourself from local competition. For example, you might choose to include a "free" (that is, included in the bundled price) follow-up 20-minute phone call or Skype meeting with each of your classes.

DISCOUNTS

Discounts can take the form of sales, reduced rates for groups, or a savings to the student for prepayment. There's a powerful psychology behind discounting because it combines the signal of a higher price (what the product or service is "worth") with a lower price for the consumer (making it more affordable, but without seeming "cheap"). When discounts are time-limited, students have an incentive to make a fast purchase.

ALIGNING YOUR PRICES

Your pricing approach should align with all of the work you did in Section 1: Getting Started. For instance, if you plan to focus on teaching professional women in a retreat format, you might find that prestige pricing is a great fit. If you prefer to teach ongoing classes, you might find that bundled pricing (students can get 10 classes for the price of 9, for example) is a solid approach.

WHAT ABOUT PRICING AT VENUES?

When working with venues, such as a craft shop, a continuing education organization, or a fiber festival, you will often have less flexibility about pricing than when you teach private lessons. Some organizations will have established pricing and payment guidelines for teachers, so you will have to decide whether those prices and payments work for you. (If you've gone through the income target exercise, this should be easy to do.)

Here are some common approaches to teacher payment in these settings:

- Hire teachers as part-time employees and pay a fixed hourly rate.
- Work with teachers as independent contractors and pay teachers...
    - A percentage of the class registration fees paid by students.
    - A fixed amount for each student who takes the class.
    - A set price for the class, including supplies and/or travel costs.
    - A fixed hourly rate for each class and a separate reimbursement for supplies.

Sometimes, these approaches are flexible and open to negotiation. In that case, having confidence and having a clear understanding of your strengths as a teacher can be your allies in obtaining a more desirable fee. In other cases, the price and teacher payments are non-negotiable, and you will need to decide whether to "take it or leave it."

> CRO-PRO TIP: Before you decide teaching at a particular venue is, or isn't, right for you, be sure to look at the **total compensation and support system** available in that setting.
>
> For example, I taught at one venue where I had to make my own copies on an old fax machine, do all of my own marketing, and set up the classroom (including carrying, setting up, and breaking down folding tables and chairs). While, on the surface, this venue paid more per hour than another site, at the other site I just had to email my handouts to the class coordinator a few days in advance, show up, and teach the class. The second venue handled all the marketing, set up the room for me, and produced collated handouts for students. I spent significantly less time in preparation and teaching at the second site, and so my hourly income was actually higher.
>
> Similarly, be sure to consider the venue's **class cancellation policy** and assess realistically the impact this policy can have on your income. For example, some craft stores will offer the teacher 100% of course registration fees (because they expect to make money on the supplies that students will buy at the shop), but cancel courses only 24 to 48 hours in advance if registration is low. Since you are unlikely to be able to schedule a class of comparable size within a few days, you may prefer to earn a lower percentage or a fixed dollar amount in exchange for having students pre-register. This allows you to have a guaranteed income (or enough time to organize a private class) rather than a potentially high income that doesn't pan out.

ONE FINAL NOTE ON PRICING

Keep in mind that prices aren't set in stone. In general, if you have very high demand for your classes, your prices are probably too low. By raising prices, you can reduce the demand by teaching fewer students (or fewer classes) and still earn the same amount of money. On the other hand, if you are having difficulty filling your classes, your prices might be too high, or you might need to improve your marketing. You can find marketing tips and tools in Section 4: Marketing.

PRICING NOTES

What's the current price range for crochet lessons (or related crafts classes in your area)?

Private lessons at local yarn shops/crafts stores: _____

Group lessons at local yarn shops/crafts stores: _____

Group lessons at "big box" stores: _____

Private lessons by private teachers: _____

Group lessons in adult education settings: _____

Other class types and settings: _____

_____

_____

_____

_____

What pricing strategies most align with your goals? _____
_____
_____
_____
_____

Based on your market research, preferred pricing strategy, and goals, how much will you charge for your private classes? _____
_____
_____
_____
_____

Will you use a different approach for classes at venues? _____
_____
_____
_____
_____

Additional pricing notes: _____
_____
_____
_____
_____
_____

SALES AND SELF-EMPLOYMENT TAXES

As I mentioned earlier, I'm neither an attorney nor an accountant, but I do know that crochet teachers are often responsible for collecting and remitting sales tax to their locality or state (especially when they sell supplies in addition to teaching) as well as paying self-employment taxes on their earnings.

If you're reading this book, you may have a DIY approach to your business, so I would urge you to start by visiting your state's taxation department website. Most have answers to frequently asked questions (FAQs) that can help you to determine if you are required to collect sales tax. If you can't find an answer, try the telephone hotline or email helpline. It's likely that you will spend a while on hold or wait a few weeks for a response, but that might be preferable to hiring an accountant.

If you have a phone conversation that confirms you do not need to collect sales tax for your classes, be sure to take note of the date and the name of the counselor in case you need to refer to this information later. Similarly, save the email or print the webpage with that same information.

If you do need to collect sales taxes, applying for a sales tax certificate is generally free and only mildly annoying. It does help to have an employer identification number (EIN), which is available for free to registered businesses in the U.S. You can learn more about applying for your EIN from the Internal Revenue Service (IRS) in Section 5: Resources.

WHAT ABOUT SELF-EMPLOYMENT TAXES?

Just as employees have taxes deducted from their paychecks, self-employed people (like most crochet teachers) are expected to pay income taxes. You can pay these quarterly (based on estimates from the prior year's income) or with your income taxes in April (though you could face a financial penalty for not prepaying throughout the year). Again, you can spend some time combing through the IRS website or calling a hotline for more details. You can find more information in Section 5: Resources.

> CRO-PRO TIP: Think about taxes when it isn't "tax season." Phone lines are often incredibly overwhelmed in February, March, and April. Ask your basic tax business questions at different times of the year for faster responses.

TAX NOTES

Local taxation office website: _____

Local taxation office phone number: _____

Your business sales tax certificate # (if applicable): _____

Employer Identification Number (EIN): _____

Notes on local sales tax: _____

_____
_____
_____
_____
_____
_____
_____
_____
_____

Notes on self-employment taxes: _____

_____
_____
_____
_____
_____
_____
_____
_____
_____

SECTION 3:
MARKETING (IT'S NOT A DIRTY WORD)

What do you think about when you hear the word "marketing"? If it fills you with dread or makes your skin crawl, read this section! You can be authentic and ethical while marketing, and it's as easy as sharing your passion with your prospective students and class coordinators.

MARKETING 101

If you haven't studied marketing in the past, you probably are not familiar with the "4 P's" of marketing: product, place, price, and promotion.

PRODUCT

As a teacher, your **product** is probably a service–teaching a class. It's helpful to think of each class in your repertoire as one product in your service line. For example, you might offer three products: a two-hour drop-in crochet class at your local yarn shop; a four-week, eight-hour Crochet 101 class at a community center; and a customizable one-hour private lesson in the student's home.

You might also choose to consider yourself–your brand as a crochet teacher–as the product because you are a generalist or because you prefer to customize your classes to the specific audience rather than developing a set menu of course options.

PLACE

In this context, **place** refers to where your classes are available to students. You might teach through one venue or at multiple locations. You might teach face-to-face courses or online courses or both.

PRICE

In Show Me the Money, we reviewed several pricing strategies you should consider. Your **price** might be consistent for each class and venue, or you might have several different price points across your service line.

PROMOTION

Promotion is how you get the word out about your classes (the product), how students can access them (the place), and the price. This is the part that most people associate with marketing. In order to promote your product effectively, you will want to know about the prospective students you are targeting and how you or your classes differ from your competition. Use this information to create messages promoting your products.

TARGET AUDIENCE

Back in Section 1: Getting Started, you thought about the students you want to teach. In some cases, those prospective students are the target audience for your promotion; but, in other cases, someone else is the decision maker. If you plan to teach children, you will need to focus your promotional activity on their parents or caretakers, for example.

Take a moment to think about the target audience members (who may or may not be your prospective students) for your marketing efforts and what you know about them:

Where do they hang out (in real life or online)? _____
_____
_____
_____

MAKE MONEY TEACHING CROCHET

What are they interested in? Is crochet already on their "to do" list, or will you have to introduce them to it? _____
_____
_____
_____
_____

What problems do they have that crochet might solve? For example, are they stressed out, lonely, frustrated, looking to rebuild fine motor skills, or trying to find a healthy activity for their residents?
_____
_____
_____
_____

Are they part of the crochet or fiber arts community online or locally already? If not, would they want to be part of that community or to stay separate? _____
_____
_____
_____
_____

> CRO-PRO TIP: If your target audience is composed of class coordinators at educational venues, consider whether a direct approach–like an introduction letter or phone call–would work best. You would likely need to do some research to find the best contact person.

YOUR COMPETITIVE ADVANTAGE

In today's world, even if you live in a community with few options for learning crochet, everyone has access to at least one great crochet teacher (as well as many terrible crochet teachers) online. It's important to think about what makes classes taught by you different from or better than those taught by someone else.

Think through some of your preferences from Section 1: Getting Started and what you know about your target audience as you consider your competitive advantage. **Alignment is always better than randomness in marketing.** For example, if you want to teach professionals in an office setting, your marketing target audience would include the human resources department of a large business in your area. Your competitive advantage may be that you present yourself professionally or have a corporate background.

COMPETITIVE ADVANTAGE WORKSHEET

Understanding your competitive advantage will help you build the confidence to negotiate with class coordinators and market your classes to your preferred student population. Use this worksheet to refine your definition of your competitive advantage. While it's always helpful to have one clear statement about your competitive advantage, if you work with several distinctive student populations, you may find it helpful to complete multiple worksheets.

Who are your ideal students? Describe them in detail! _____
_____
_____
_____
_____
_____
_____
_____

What problems or concerns do your ideal students have that crochet classes could help solve? _____
_____
_____
_____
_____
_____
_____

Is there is another person, such as a parent, teacher, store manager, or class coordinator, that you need to communicate with to reach your ideal students? If so, what problems and concerns does this person have that a crochet class could solve? _____
_____
_____
_____
_____
_____
_____

What makes you different from other crochet teachers? What do you do differently or better (or more or less) than other teachers to solve these problems of your students (or their intermediaries)? If you specialize in a type of class, location, or technique, don't forget to include that! _____

Draft a competitive advantage statement to use as an introduction. Keep it brief and conversational but include the students you work with, how you solve their problems or concerns, and any specializations you may have. _____

MARKETING OPTIONS

Now that you've thought through the 4 P's, your competitive advantage, and your target audience, let's discuss some places you might promote your classes or business.

ONLINE

Establishing an online presence can definitely help with promotion.

Website. Your own website can serve as a hub for your marketing efforts, an online business card for prospective students or class coordinators, and a tool in your educational arsenal. If you don't already have your own website, there are many free and affordable options available. You can find some options in Section 5: Resources.

- **Social Media Platforms.** Regardless of your own website, social media platforms allow you to promote your classes for free or at low cost. There are many social networks (and more emerging each day), so here are a few options to consider. As social media platforms are frequently evolving, consider establishing yourself on one platform before adopting another. Here are a few options to consider:

- **Facebook.** Facebook is the largest social network in the world. On Facebook, you can use your personal profile, but I recommend setting up a page for your teaching (or crochet) business. You can promote your classes as events or via your status updates. With Facebook Live, you can stream live videos through your page and directly or indirectly promote upcoming classes. Facebook offers many affordable advertising options, too. If you offer regular drop-in classes at a set location, you can also list those as your "hours" on Facebook. Find more information about these options in Section 5: Resources.

- **LinkedIn.** LinkedIn is distinguished from other social networks because it emphasizes professional networking. You can include your crochet résumé in your profile, share information about upcoming classes as status updates, and publish articles about crochet (as new content or reprints of work you've published elsewhere). You can also research class coordinators of teaching venues here. Find more information about these options in Section 5: Resources.

- **Ravelry.** Hopefully, if you are planning to teach crochet, you are already aware of Ravelry, a social network for yarn lovers, and are a member, too. You can post about classes in an existing group and/or create your own group so your fans can hear about your latest classes, designs, and creations. Ravelry also has extremely affordable advertising options, which you can target for groups in a specific geographic area or with an interest in specialty techniques, for example. Find more information about these options in Section 5: Resources.

- **Instagram.** Instagram is a photo-sharing social network that is available only as a mobile application. Posting inspiring pictures with proper use of hashtags can help you to connect with prospective students in a local area or with an interest in a particular technique. You can also advertise on Instagram affordably. Find more information about these options in Section 5: Resources.

- **Twitter.** Twitter is a popular social network for journalists and bloggers, so you may find it helps you to get your name out through networking with local and needlecrafts reporters and bloggers. Again, proper use of hashtags for your local area may help. Twitter has advertising options, too; but, from what I've heard, they may not be so effective for microbusinesses. Find more information about these options in Section 5: Resources.

- **YouTube.** YouTube is a video-sharing platform, a social network, and the second-largest search engine in the world. Teachers can use YouTube for online classes, introductory videos, or a sample "speaking reel" for class coordinators. Find more information about these options in Section 5: Resources.

Social media platforms change frequently, and most, including those mentioned already and Pinterest, are adding affordable advertising options that could help you find students for your classes. My favorite source for keeping abreast of the latest changes and their impact on marketing is Social Media Examiner. You can find more information about it in Section 5: Resources.

OTHER ONLINE MARKETING RESOURCES

Online promotion is often more affordable than local advertising, and it's frequently much easier to track the success of a particular campaign. For these reasons, online advertising is a great option for crochet teachers.

Besides Facebook and Ravelry ads (and Instagram, Pinterest, and Twitter ads), some other options to consider are Craigslist (if available in your local area), ClassClassifieds, and TakeLessons. You can find more information about these sites in Section 5: Resources. Here are some more ideas:

- Sign up for *Help a Reporter Out* (HARO) and respond to media requests for expertise. Think outside the box here and consider all of the "hats" you wear when responding. You might respond to a request for a mom, a small business owner, or someone who can speak about relaxing activities in your local community. Though few reporters are writing articles about how great crochet is, you might get the opportunity to build a reputation and get the word out about your classes. You can learn more about HARO in Section 5: Resources.
- Consider pitching ideas for *guest posts or articles for local newspapers, websites, and blogs*. Building your authority as a teacher locally can help you to promote your services. For best results, do your homework on the site before sending in your pitch, and think about what you will offer to the site's readers. This isn't advertising, so a guest post about why someone should take your classes is probably not very valuable for most bloggers. However, a post about how crochet can be a healthy stress-relief outlet for teens might be a great fit for a parenting blog. This same approach can be used for podcasts.
- Start an *email list* and share information about upcoming classes, crochet tips and tutorials, news about your business, or other information with your subscribers. You can learn more about starting and growing an email list in Section 5: Resources.

GOOD OLE-FASHIONED PUBLIC RELATIONS (P.R.)

Let's not forget about the regular old, pre-Internet ways of spreading the word about your classes:

- **Word of Mouth.** Satisfied students can spread the word about your classes faster than most other methods. Invite students to join your email list and share it with friends. Offer a referral discount for private classes to incentivize current students to talk with friends and take more classes with you.
- **Testimonials.** You may also want to ask your satisfied students for testimonials or reviews to share on your website or in other marketing materials. Consider asking very satisfied students to be references. You can demonstrate social proof that your classes are worthwhile by sharing these experiences with prospective students.
- **Local Press.** Classified advertising or clearly written press releases to your local paper can help spread the word about your classes.
- **Local Crochet Guild of America Chapters or craft groups.** Your local CGOA chapter may allow members to list their classes in their newsletters. They may also allow you to teach mini-lessons at their meetings or pay you to teach classes at their events. Find more information about CGOA chapters in Section 5: Resources.
- **Fliers.** Remember those paper things? Yep, a concise and attractive flier can help recruit students. You might post it in a community center, a large workplace, your local library, a college, or another setting where you think it could reach potential students. Be sure to follow guidelines for posting fliers in your community or at venues to avoid fines.
- **Alumni Groups and Membership Organizations.** Don't forget to talk about your teaching as you interact with other organizations where you already have an established reputation (even if it isn't as a crocheter). People may already trust you in these settings, so now you just have to convince them that they want to learn to crochet.

THE TEACHING VENUE

If you are partnering with an organization or site to offer classes, they will often be involved with recruitment as well. The expectations about student recruitment should be discussed when establishing the connection. For example, are you as the teacher responsible for all advertising, a portion, or none at all (except what you do anyway because you are an awesome professional crochet teacher)?

If the organization is taking responsibility for advertising your classes, look over their materials. Are you being presented accurately? Do the classes sound interesting? Perhaps you can provide pictures or a bio, which would be helpful for recruitment, even if you do not have the ultimate responsibility for bringing in students.

> CRO-PRO TIP: Learn from the world's largest retailers and think seasonally when scheduling and marketing your classes. It's hard to draw a big crowd for that class on making your own sweater in chunky yarns during the hottest months. Try to plan your seasonal marketing so that your classes are offered about six weeks before the event (unless it is a "last-minute projects" theme). This will allow your students time to finish the projects started in class. As an example, early November would be a great time to start a series of project classes for winter holiday gifts. Tracking trends on Pinterest is a great way to watch seasonal marketing trends. You can find more information in Section 5: Resources.

PROMOTIONAL ITEMS

You might want to consider using affordable promotional items to market your business, too. Consider these ideas:

- Distribute supplies with your business name on them to students in class to help with word-of-mouth marketing. Rulers, pens, or bamboo crochet hooks are easily customized.
- Carry business cards wherever you go, especially when crocheting in public. When people ask questions, as they inevitably will, you can give them a business card. (It goes without saying that wearing what you have crocheted is also a great conversation starter.)

Think about whether it makes sense for you to make some branded items- like a tote bag, bumper magnet, or water bottle-to bring with you to class to reinforce your business name with students. Find more information about promotional items in Section 5: Resources.

DO FREE SAMPLES WORK?

I don't generally recommend distributing handmade items as a way of promoting your teaching business for several reasons. When you actually consider the cost of your own labor and materials, you'll find that you're spending a lot on advertising. Your handmade samples may also be targeting the wrong audience. There are more people who like to wear handmade items than there are people who want to pay to learn to crochet those items.

However, if you do decide to provide free samples, here are ways to improve the return on your investment:

- **Find an influencer.** If you are going to invest the time, effort, and expense in creating free projects, make sure you choose the recipient wisely. Ideally, it will be someone who can convince other people to take your classes! This person should be respected, admired, or of interest to your target audience, too.
- **Offer mini-classes.** Offering a free sample of your teaching is more likely to result in meeting students than offering a free sample of your crochet skills. You may be able to partner with a venue to offer free mini-classes at no cost to you. Consider going to a "knit in public" event (since these are generally open to crocheters, too), health fair, block party, or other community activity and teaching a simple and easy "make and take" project, like a chain bracelet.
- **Combine both concepts!** Offer a free class to local influencers. They will be able to talk about how great you are as a teacher and make a project to show off. If you teach online, you can reach out to influencers beyond your local area.

WHAT ABOUT COURSE DESCRIPTIONS?

While course descriptions are part of your preparation for a class, it's helpful to think about them from a marketing standpoint, too. You should consider writing two versions—a description for you, which includes things like the objectives, project notes, and other details that will help you prepare; and a marketing description, which entices people to take the class.

In writing your course description for marketing purposes, remember that crochet classes aren't usually something people "need" to take, but rather something they want to do. Think about how the class might solve a problem, or tell a story to help create interest among your prospective students.

Many teachers find that it is effective to start the course description with a question or problem ("Are you tired of crocheting sweaters that don't fit?") and then sharing how the class can provide answers or solutions ("Make all of your color changes invisible with this simple trick.").

> CRO-PRO TIP: Look at the descriptions other successful teachers use. Of course, you shouldn't copy other teachers' course descriptions, but you might find it useful to adapt them in your own voice. Look at the websites for the larger regional and national fiber conferences for inspiration, like the CGOA Conference, Pittsburgh Knit & Crochet Show, STITCHES, or Rhinebeck. Find more information about these shows in Section 5: Resources.

Finally, create a template for the less exciting (but still pertinent) details about each class, including the time and date(s), location, required supplies, skills needed, price, and any homework, so you don't forget to include this information with each description. A sample class description template is available as Appendix A.

A FINAL NOTE

If considering the many options is making marketing seem too overwhelming, start slowly and focus on just one or two options. (This is especially true if your crochet business is a part-time job for you.) You can always expand once you feel more comfortable, or switch to other options if you aren't satisfied with the results.

You can also outsource your marketing. Some teachers work exclusively with venues with a strong marketing presence for this very reason. Others bring in a local or remote virtual assistant and delegate marketing activities.

I always recommend that teachers start and maintain an email list, even if it is used only to announce upcoming courses. **If you take just one step to market your teaching business, set up an email list!**

MARKETING NOTES

Use this space to track your marketing efforts, including outreach to local media and influencers, ad placements, and more!

SECTION 4: PREPPING FOR CLASS

Now that you've refined your teaching preferences and updated your skills, set your prices and policies, and marketed your courses, the big day has arrived — you know, the one where you actually start teaching. This section will focus on preparing for class so you can deliver a great experience for your students while enjoying yourself.

THE BIG PICTURE: SESSION AND COURSE PREPARATION

Begin your preparation for each class session or multi-session course by taking a step back to look at the overall *learning objectives for the students* and to ask yourself these questions:

- Is there a particular skill or set of skills you want the students to master by the end of class?
- Is there a project the students should finish by the end of class?
- If a project can't be finished in class, are there additional skills, tips, or information students will need to learn in class so they can successfully finish the project at home?

While it's tempting to have grandiose plans for every class you teach, be aware that some students in every class will struggle. For that reason, I find it helpful to have three tiers of objectives for each of my class sessions. For example, I teach a 10-week beginner crochet class at a local union. For the first session, here are the learning objectives I use:

- All students: Learn to hold the hook and yarn and make a chain.
- Fast learners: Learn to make a single crochet.
- Students with previous preparation: Learn to crochet in front loop only, back loop only, and under both loops. Practice even tension. Understand turning chains.

At the same time, there will be other students who are moving much faster than everyone else. I over-prepare by bringing additional printed materials for these students, especially since they can sometimes disrupt a class where slower learners need more attention. I bring crochet books with me to class so that more advanced students can browse for projects, learn more about yarn, or read about a new technique that I can help them learn at their own pace. Additional handouts can also help.

For a multi-session course, start by outlining your objectives for the entire series. Then, work backwards to figure out which objectives are appropriate for specific sessions. A sample learning objectives template is available as Appendix B.

MAKE MONEY TEACHING CROCHET

CRO-PRO TIP: Keep in mind that short-term memory can hold only about seven items at a time. To a beginner, a single stitch may have seven components! As an example, a beginner may be thinking this way:

1. Hold the hook in my dominant hand.

2. Keep my thumb on the thumb rest.

3. Hold the yarn in my other hand.

4. Don't hold the yarn too tight.

5. Wrap the yarn around my crochet hook from the back to the front.

6. Pull the yarn through the loop on the hook.

A more advanced crocheter will simply think "make a chain" and will have "room" in their short-term memory for six additional steps.

Use this information in your teaching! Limit learning objectives for beginner crochet classes so students can repeat steps often enough to move the multi-step process into long-term memory. While students often want to push through content very quickly (especially in private lessons where they want to "get the most bang for their buck"), encourage them to repeat new skills so they can retain the information after class.

Once you have your objectives set for a particular class session, **_outline everything you'll need to teach_**. As you prepare your classes for the very first time, more detail is probably better than less. When I first started teaching, I would write out multi-page lesson plans including two or three ways to explain each skill (e.g., how to make a slip knot). Writing out detailed descriptions can help you build your teaching confidence since you'll know that you have at least two or three ways to explain something to a confused student. You can also refer back to your lesson plan during class if you get flustered or off track. (By the way, now I find a simple bulleted list of topics is enough preparation for a class I've taught before.) A sample class outline template is available as Appendix C.

Once you've developed your learning objectives and outline or lesson plan, you can think about the details of what to bring to each class session.

COURSE PREP: SHOULD YOU SAMPLE OR SWATCH?

In my experience, teachers are pretty divided about whether to bring completed projects or swatches demonstrating techniques and stitches to class. Let's consider each approach:

- Completed samples give students visual cues about the project. For students who have difficulty visualizing things, a sample project is a great way to make the project "real." Completed projects can also help students who are very visual explore how and where they might make alterations.
- On the other hand, completed samples take longer to make, are more supply-intensive, and are more difficult to store. Samples can sometimes be intimidating to beginner students, who might compare your perfect sample to their disheveled stitches and get discouraged.
- Swatches are easier to make, store, and carry. You can often use the same swatch for a broad range of classes, making swatches more versatile than full samples. Swatches are much less intimidating to beginner students because the small size makes the project seem more achievable.
- On the other hand, it can be difficult for students (especially inexperienced crocheters) to visualize a completed project from a swatch. Swatches often need to be supplemented with photos and schematics.

I personally lean towards swatching. In my early days of teaching, I had some experiences where I created samples for classes I didn't even end up teaching. Once you start teaching, I recommend taking pictures of all of your projects. This allows you to supplement swatches with photos, without needing to make another sample.

> CRO-PRO TIP: Create a photo album for your classes. Bring it to class as an album in your phone, tablet, or other electronic device, or make a portfolio book, using a service like Blurb or Mixbook. Portfolio books make a great impression on prospective class coordinators, too. Find more information about portfolio options in Section 5: Resources.

PREP IN ADVANCE: PACKING FOR CLASS

If you offer more than one class, as most crochet teachers do, you may find that you occasionally arrive at class without all of your materials. This can be frustrating for you and your students, and it also gives the impression that you are disorganized and/or unprofessional. For this reason, I create a packing list (or a separate packed bag) for each course that I teach. Here are some items you should likely include on your packing list for every class you teach:

- *Folder for handouts, sign-in sheets, receipts, and other materials.* If the course has multiple sessions, pocket folders are best.
- *Pencil or pen and notepad or blank/scrap paper.* You might need a place to jot down notes (like student names in a seating chart) during class, or to add reminders to yourself for upcoming sessions. You could also take notes on your phone or tablet, but students sometimes think it rude when instructors use their electronic devices during class.
- *Class outline or notes.* Having an outline or list of topics for class is very helpful for keeping you on track, especially if you are teaching a class for the first time or have a larger-than-expected audience.

- *Scissors, gauge ruler, tape measure, yarn needles, and stitch markers.* Students often forget to bring notions to class, so it can be helpful to carry extras to lend out. Notions can also be used in class for demonstrations.
- *Watch or alarm clock.* Because some students (especially older students) may feel it is rude for a teacher to look at her/his phone during class, consider bringing a watch or small alarm clock to keep your class pacing on target.
- *Yarn and hooks.* In some class settings, students frequently come unprepared. I often ball up leftover yarn and bring some inexpensive hooks with me so I can lend (or give) them to students during class. And, of course, you should bring your own yarn and hook(s) for demonstrations.

> CRO-PRO TIP: Choose light yarn colors and a contrasting hook for demonstration. This makes it easier for students to observe what you are doing, even when lighting conditions aren't perfect. Some teachers find that using larger hooks and thick yarn for demonstrations makes it easier for students to see what you are doing.

- *Swatches, samples, and/or portfolio images.* You might have a general set that you bring to every class or customize these for specific classes.
- *Business cards.* While some venues prohibit marketing in class, students will often ask for private lessons or more information about your other services. It is generally permissible to share a business card at the student's request.
- *Mailing list sign-up sheet.* Again, many venues prohibit teachers from marketing other services and products in class, but allow you to pass around a mailing list sign-up sheet. Be sure to comply with your country's laws for email marketing by providing double opt-ins for your mailing list, if necessary.
- *Personal hygiene kit.* This is especially critical when you are teaching long classes or classes at a new-to-you venue.

> CRO-PRO TIP: I keep a personal hygiene kit in my teaching tool bag that includes a nail file and clippers, moisturizer, hand sanitizer, tissues, small bandages, lip balm, toothpaste, and a toothbrush.

MAKE MONEY TEACHING CROCHET

- *Promotional items.* Some teachers find it helpful to provide branded freebies to students so they remember your contact information outside of class. Over the years, I've given students crochet hooks, Tunisian crochet hooks, acrylic rulers, and pencils with my business name. Most venues allow these types of giveaways, especially if they are not accompanied by a marketing pitch or if they are part of a supply kit. - Section 5: Resources includes some of the websites I recommend for purchasing promotional items.
- *Bottled water.* If the venue where you teach has a water fountain or a water cooler, you can substitute an empty water bottle.
- *Snack.* A banana, granola bar, trail mix, or any snack that can be eaten quickly without much mess is ideal.
- *Handouts.* Remember to include your business contact information on any handouts you develop. If using handouts developed by another organization, be sure to get permission before distribution.

> CRO-PRO TIP: If you aren't developing your own handouts, be sure to obey copyright laws. When I started teaching, I contacted several yarn companies and asked for permission to copy and distribute their patterns as handouts in my classes. Most granted me permission as long as I didn't alter their patterns. Keep an archived copy of any such emails for future reference.

> CRO-PRO TIP: Today, you can go paperless for your classes, but many students will still want access to reference materials from home. Consider setting up a special link on your website (e.g., yourbusinessname.com/students or yourbusinessname.com/class/handout) where students can download class handouts or find links to helpful tutorials or patterns. This is also a great way to get sign-ups to your mailing list! You can write the link on a flip chart or whiteboard in the classroom, or keep the back of your business cards blank and then write in (or add a label with) a custom link to distribute in class. You can find more information about creating custom links in Section 5: Resources.

- 🧶 **Evaluations.** Some venues have student evaluations that they ask teachers to distribute or that are sent to students after the class. You might also want to consider developing a short set of questions to ask students after class in order to improve your teaching and to get ideas for upcoming classes.

Developing your packing list for the first time will be time consuming, but it can be used over and over again whenever you teach that class (and it can be modified for other classes). So take the time to do it well. A sample packing list template is available as Appendix D.

DAY OF THE CLASS: PERSONAL PREPARATION

To build a solid reputation as a teacher and to have the most energy for dealing with the unexpected, prepare for your classes by attending to your personal needs beforehand. This preparation includes the following:

- 🧶 *Getting adequate sleep the night before.* Being well rested and appearing energetic is an important way to establish your authority and confidence in the class. Teachers who look exhausted (or yawn during class) often appear disheveled, disorganized, or rude to students.
- 🧶 *Eating beforehand.* While most venues will permit teachers to bring water into the classroom, any eating should be done before class begins. Not only will this give you adequate time to use the restroom if necessary, but also will keep you from scaring students off by talking to them with food in your teeth.
- 🧶 *Attending to personal hygiene.* As a crochet teacher, you may need to get into very close personal proximity to your students—leaning over their shoulders or holding their hands while they work, for example. Be particularly attentive to your hands (including cleaning under the fingernails, moisturizing the skin, and covering any wounds) and your breath.
- 🧶 *Using the restroom before class.* In most instances, it will be inappropriate for the teacher to take a "bio break" during class. Even in longer classes with a break, you might find it difficult to leave the room if students have questions. For this reason, always use the restroom before class.

- *Wearing venue-appropriate clothing.* When you teach through a venue, you are part of the team and should dress according to the professional standards of that organization. When teaching private lessons, consider the most appropriate clothing for your target audience.

BUT, WHAT IF YOU'RE TEACHING ONLINE?

Whether you're developing an online video course that you can earn passive income from or offering private lessons via Skype, Google Hangouts, or another live video chat service, there are some additional steps you might want to take to get prepared:

- **Invest in a microphone.** While video is often thought of as a purely visual medium, audio quality is very important. Upgrade from the built-in microphone on your recording device if you plan to do a pre-recorded series or offer frequent live classes. I use an affordable USB microphone, the Blue Snowball, for recording from my laptop, and an inexpensive lavaliere, the Audio Technica ATR3350, when recording from my DSLR camera. If you will be using your mobile device for recording, I've heard good things about the Audio Technica ATR2100, though I've never used it. Cleaning your mouth, drinking water, and wearing lip balm, combined with placing yourself at the proper angle and distance from your microphone, will go a long way towards improving your audio quality.
- **Consider lighting.** If you will be demonstrating crochet techniques in your videos, strong lighting will help your students see the details of your hand movements, tools, or stitches. There are many affordable tabletop lighting options available through Adorama, Amazon, and other retailers, or you can create a DIY set-up.
- **Minimize distractions.** To keep your students or prospective students focused on your videos, minimize distractions by limiting what's viewable in the background, limiting background noises, and staying focused.

> CRO-PRO TIP: If you're using wired microphones, be sure to place any items you plan to use during your video away from the cords to avoid accidents.

For live streaming video, I recommend placing a list of talking points close to the camera so you can maintain as much eye contact with your audience as possible while periodically glancing at your outline to be sure you haven't missed any major topics. Similarly, place any materials you plan to use within arm's reach so you don't have to step off camera at any point.

> CRO-PRO TIP: Always try out a streaming platform before your first workshop or live event. Use a Skype Test Call, try Facebook Live on your personal page, or hold a Google Hangout with a friend to get familiar with the settings and interface before your first class or event.

For pre-recorded videos, a little editing can help a lot! Adding title cards, removing "dead air," and adjusting volume levels can really improve the experience for your student viewers.

As when teaching face-to-face classes, you'll want to customize your preparation list for video sessions to include details like turning off the ringer on your phone or closing the closet door. You can find more information about video classes in Section 5: Resources.

I STARTED TEACHING. NOW WHAT?

Once you've started teaching (or re-launched your teaching business), here are four things I recommend doing regularly to keep your business on track and growing.

REVIEW YOUR GOALS PERIODICALLY

Now that you've started teaching, go back monthly or quarterly to goals you set in Section 1: Getting Started to review your short- and long-term goals for your teaching business. In the day-to-day wackiness of teaching, it's easy to lose sight of your bigger goals.

You may want to make adjustments to your goals based on your experiences or make changes to your teaching to bring you into better alignment with your goals.

ANALYZE WHAT'S WORKING—AND WHAT ISN'T

It's a good idea to analyze both your marketing efforts and your teaching at least quarterly.

For your marketing efforts, analyze what methods have worked for you, using these ideas:

- Create slightly different links for each online marketing method you use so you can track the number of clicks from that source and see which sources convert into class sales. You can learn more about link tracking in Section 5: Resources.
- Ask students, "How did you hear about this class?"

If you find that certain marketing methods aren't working for you, consider investing more money and time in the methods that are working well or re-tooling those other methods to improve conversion.

Similarly, look over your course evaluations to see what needs improvement as well as what students are enjoying. You may find some great ideas for new classes from your existing satisfied students, too. A sample course evaluation template is available as Appendix E.

TRACK TRENDS

It doesn't hurt to stay on top of the latest trends in crochet, fashion, and home decor, even if you don't plan to teach courses specifically on trending topics. Check for trends using Ravelry's Hot Right Now list in crochet and Amazon's Best Sellers in Crochet (sadly, some of this list will be knitting) or through a crochet search on Pinterest or BuzzSumo. Pantone releases free color trend reports at least twice a year. Using trending colors for samples and marketing materials can help give a fresh look to your classes. You can find more information on tracking trends in Section 5: Resources.

UPDATE AND REFRESH

I also encourage **you** to stay fresh as a teacher by regularly taking classes and reading books to develop your skills further. While it's tempting to feel like there is nothing more to learn because you're an expert, there are always new things to learn in crochet. You may find that learning a new technique, trying a different type of project, or just hearing how another teacher explains something can provide a breath of fresh air to your teaching so that it doesn't become stale.

And, of course, there is always more to learn about the business side of things, especially in the ever-shifting world of social media and online marketing.

Good luck in expanding your crochet teaching business!

SECTION 5: RESOURCES

HELPFUL SITES AND TOOLS

Throughout the book, I've mentioned helpful websites and tools. In this section, I'm sharing more details and links to these resources as well as a few others you might want to use. Links followed by an asterisk (*) are affiliate links, meaning that I might earn a small commission at no extra cost to you if you make a purchase using one of them.

BUSINESS BANKING

Microbusinesses are generally best served by community banks rather than by multinational banks. Community banks are smaller and independently owned. Their missions explicitly include supporting the local economy and small businesses. Community banks usually have no- or low-fee business checking accounts and may offer other services to microbusinesses. My business banking account is with Popular Community Bank https://www.popularcommunitybank.com/. You can find out more about community banks, as well as a community bank locator, at the Independent Community Bankers of America site http://www.icba.org/.

CUSTOM LINKS (TRACKABLE LINKS)

To better track your marketing efforts, you may want to set up custom links. As an example, you can list your website as YourBusinessName.com/localpaper in an ad in the local paper and as YourBusinessName.com/Instagram on Instagram.

- If you use WordPress, Pretty Link Lite https://wordpress.org/plugins/pretty-link/ is a free plugin that makes it easy for you to customize links for your domain.
- If you don't use WordPress (or don't have a website), consider using Bit.ly https://bitly.com/pages/tour, a link shortener that allows you to track your links. While the links won't be as branded, they will be short and trackable.

EMAIL MARKETING

I believe every crochet teacher should set up an email list to connect with current, former, and prospective students. Sending out mass emails from your email account is a great way to get your account shut down or blocked as spam, so use an email service. I've personally used three different companies over the years, and I recommend all of them:

- **Mad Mimi** https://madmimi.com/ is very straightforward and simple to use, even for "technophobic" teachers. You can start with a free account and then upgrade once you grow your list.
- **MailChimp** http://mailchimp.com/ is a bit more complicated to use, but is still manageable. You can also start with a free account and then upgrade to a paid account later.
- **Feedblitz** http://www.feedblitz.com/ offers free RSS subscription management, which sends an email to your subscribers when you update your blog. They also have a range of pricing options for email newsletter management. The company is very hands on and will walk you through the process of getting set up at no additional charge. There is a 30-day free trial.

Remember that you can always switch your email list manager and transfer your subscribers later as your business grows or your needs change. For more information about getting started with email, listen to this episode of the Creative Yarn Entrepreneur Show: **Episode 55: Email Marketing 101: Or, Why and How to Set Up an Email List for Your Creative Business** http://creativeyarnentrepreneur.com/episode55

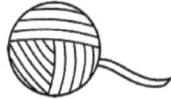

FIBER FESTIVALS

Fiber festivals can be great ways to stay inspired, take new classes, and network with other crocheters. Once you have more experience teaching, you may even consider submitting a proposal to teach! Here are a few crochet-friendly events to consider.

- Knit and Crochet Show http://www.knitandcrochetshow.com/
- New York State Sheep and Wool Festival (also known as Rhinebeck) http://sheepandwool.com/
- Pittsburgh Knit and Crochet Festival http://pghknitandcrochet.com/
- STITCHES regional events http://www.knittinguniverse.com/stitches/

Knitter's Review also maintains a very comprehensive calendar of international events http://www.knittersreview.com/upcoming_events.asp.

ONLINE TEACHING/VIDEO

There are many options for teaching crochet classes online. Some of the most common ways to use video for teaching are listed below:

ORGANIZE YOUR OWN LIVE 1:1 OR SMALL GROUP PRIVATE LESSON

- **Google Hangouts** https://apps.google.com/learning-center/products/hangouts/get-started/ can be used for teaching 1:1 or small group lessons online or for sharing live video broadcasts. Choose the "Hangout on Air" option https://support.google.com/plus/answer/2553119?hl=en to record a video that you can share on demand after broadcasting on a linked YouTube account.
- **Skype** https://support.skype.com/en/faq/FA10328/what-are-the-system-requirements-for-skype video calls are another option for teaching 1:1 lessons online. Skype group calls are a bit trickier to manage than Google Hangouts.

ORGANIZE AND DELIVER ONLINE CLASSES

Creating an online course that you sell and promote via your own platform allows you to maximize control over your course and earn the highest profit from each enrolled student. On the other hand, you have fewer marketing and tech support resources than when using an external platform. Check out both of these:

- **Vimeo Pro** http://creativeyarnentrepreneur.com/vimeo* is an affordable option for sharing private and password-protected videos. If you'd like to teach an online course, you can send the links to the videos to registered students via an email course or embed videos on a website where students must log in.
- **YouTube** is great for sharing free tutorials to reinforce what you've taught in face-to-face classes or to share demo lessons or a "speaker reel" with class coordinators. Learn more about YouTube in the Social Media section. (By the way, the Creator Academy https://youtube.com/creatoracademy/page/education?hl=en has many helpful resources for making videos on any platform.)

CREATE ONLINE CLASSES TO DELIVER VIA OTHER PLATFORMS

Creating an online course on an existing learning platform allows you to share marketing and tech support resources with a larger organization while earning a smaller percentage of the total sales. Here are two options:

- **Skillshare** https://www.skillshare.com/teach is an online learning community where you can share your video classes.
- **Udemy** https://teach.udemy.com/ is a large platform for online learning that allows people to create and offer their own online courses for free or for sale. They offer a free class https://www.udemy.com/official-udemy-instructor-course/ to help prospective instructors plan a new course.

COLLABORATE WITH AN ONLINE CRAFT PLATFORM

There are several online learning platforms in the crafting/creative learning space. These platforms work with instructors to develop courses in exchange for marketing support and profit sharing or for a flat rate.

If you are considering working with an online craft platform, take some classes first to see if the platform is a good fit since each one has a different style and format. While you can pitch your course ideas online, you may have more success by making a connection with the platform first as an affiliate, at an event, or through a referral. Consider these:

- Use the *CraftArtEdu* contact page http://craftartedu.com/contacts/ to start a conversation about teaching a course.
- *Craftsy* has an online course proposal form http://creativeyarnentrepreneur.com/CraftsyCourse.*
- **Craft University** has an instructor application https://www.craftonlineuniversity.com/pages/become-an-instructor.
- You can email **Creativebug** http://creativeyarnentrepreneur.com/CreativebugLLC* to recommend a prospective instructor (including yourself).

MEMBERSHIP ORGANIZATIONS

As a teaching professional, you may want to consider joining one of these membership organizations.

- Crochet Guild of America (CGOA) http://www.crochet.org/ offers associate professional and professional levels of membership.
- The National NeedleArts Association (TNNA) http://www.tnna.org/ offers several affiliate membership options. Teachers can join as Designers or Business & Creative Services members. You can learn more about the benefits of joining TNNA in this episode of the Creative Yarn Entrepreneur Show: **Episode 61: TNNA Membership and Trade Show for Newbies** http://creativeyarnentrepreneur.com/episode61/.

PAYMENT OPTIONS

There are countless options available for accepting charge/credit/debit card payments at events and for accepting payments online. Here are a few that I have used or heard good things about over the years (don't forget to ask if the bank you use for your business account has an affordable option for a merchant payment system, too):

- PayPal https://www.paypal.com/home
- ProPay http://www.propay.com/
- QuickBooks GoPayment http://quickbooks.intuit.com/payments/gopayment_product_page
- Square https://squareup.com/
- Venmo https://venmo.com/paywithvenmo/business

PORTFOLIO SERVICES

A printed portfolio can impress students and class coordinators alike. Here are two services I recommend.

- **Blurb** http://creativeyarnentrepreneur.com/Blurb* is a self-publishing site that allows you to create print or iPad and Kindle photo books and portfolios.
- **Mixbook** http://creativeyarnentrepreneur.com/Mixbook* is a tool that lets you create custom photo products, including portfolios, calendars, and cards.

PROFESSIONAL DEVELOPMENT

If you need to enhance your own skills, here are some great resources to consider:

- *Craft Yarn Council (CYC) Certified Instructors Program (CIP) in Crochet and Knitting* http://www.craftyarncouncil.com/teach.html is a certification program that is required by many of the larger craft retailers and may also provide a competitive advantage in other situations. At the time of this writing, the cost is $170 for Levels I & II as a correspondence course and $200 for an on-site class.
- *Crochet Guild of America (CGOA) Master of Advanced Crochet Stitches and Techniques* http://www.crochet.org/?MastersInfo is a correspondence program designed to improve your technical skills in crochet. At the time of this writing, the cost is $152.
- *Toastmasters* https://www.toastmasters.org/ is an international nonprofit organization dedicated to building public speaking and leadership skills through practice and feedback.

There are too many great crochet books to mention, but here are several that I have found indispensable for my own development as a crocheter and that also provide great examples of teaching:

- *The Crochet Answer Book* by Edie Eckman http://creativeyarnentrepreneur.com/crochetanswerbook* shares answers to common and uncommon crochet questions.
- *Crochet Master Class* by Jean Leinhauser and Rita Weiss http://creativeyarnentrepreneur.com/crochetmasterclass* introduces crochet techniques through the eyes of master crocheters.
- *Crochet Workshop* by James Walters http://creativeyarnentrepreneur.com/crochetworkshop* shares information about stitches and techniques as well as about design.

MAKE MONEY TEACHING CROCHET

- *The Crochet Workbook* by James Walters and Sylvia Cosh http://creativeyarnentrepreneur.com/crochetworkbook* is a great introduction to freeform crochet.
- *Couture Crochet Workshop* by Lily Chin http://creativeyarnentrepreneur.com/couturecrochet* and *Custom Crochet Sweaters* by Dora Ohrenstein http://creativeyarnentrepreneur.com/customsweaters* share great information about fitting, pattern customization, and garment design.

If you'd like to take an online course to develop your crochet, photography, teaching, or business skills, Craftsy http://creativeyarnentrepreneur.com/Craftsy* and CreativeLive http://creativeyarnentrepreneur.com/CreativeLive* are wonderful resources with thousands of affordable course options. Here are a few courses to consider:

CROCHET CLASSES

- Aran Crochet http://creativeyarnentrepreneur.com/AranCrochet*
- Beyond Basic Broomstick Lace http://creativeyarnentrepreneur.com/BBBL*
- Freeform Crochet http://creativeyarnentrepreneur.com/Freeform*
- Modern Irish Freeform Crochet http://creativeyarnentrepreneur.com/ModIrish*
- Tunisian Crochet: Revolutions in Color and Style http://creativeyarnentrepreneur.com/TC*

PHOTOGRAPHY CLASSES

- Basics of Digital Photography http://creativeyarnentrepreneur.com/BasicsDigital*
- Craft Photography Fundamentals http://creativeyarnentrepreneur.com/CraftPhoto*
- Creative iPhoneography Tips & Tricks http://creativeyarnentrepreneur.com/iPhoneography*
- Mobile Photography: Perfect Photos in Your Pocket http://creativeyarnentrepreneur.com/MobilePhoto*
- Product Photography at Home http://creativeyarnentrepreneur.com/ProductPhoto*
- Shoot It!: A Product Photography Primer http://creativeyarnentrepreneur.com/ShootIt*

MARKETING AND SMALL BUSINESS CLASSES

- Bookkeeping for Crafters http://creativeyarnentrepreneur.com/Bookkeeping*
- Creative Advertising for Small Business Owners http://creativeyarnentrepreneur.com/Ads*
- Email Marketing for Crafters http://creativeyarnentrepreneur.com/emailMtkg*
- Marketing for Crafters http://creativeyarnentrepreneur.com/MktgCraft*

PROMOTIONAL ITEMS

Creating and distributing your own promotional items is a great way to make your business seem more professional to your students and increase word-of-mouth. Think about these options:

- **Business cards**: I've used VistaPrint http://www.vistaprint.com/ and have heard great things about Moo https://www.moo.com/us/.
- **Crochet hooks**: I've bought bamboo hooks in bulk from manufacturers in China. These can be used as supplies and promo items. If you can afford only a small order, 8 Seasons http://www.8seasons.com/ is an option. If you can afford to make a larger, wholesale order, the price of each hook will drop significantly. You can connect with manufacturers through Alibaba https://www.alibaba.com/. Often, the manufacturer can laser engrave your business name on the hooks, or you can find an Etsy seller to do the same. (Have your hooks delivered straight to the Etsy seller to save on shipping and time.)
- **Inexpensive giveaway items (e.g., rulers, pens)**: I've used 4imprint https://www.4imprint.com/ for promo items for myself and other companies I've worked for in the past.
- **Personal branding and print-on-demand products**: If you'd like to create your own branded items, like T-shirts, smartphone cases, mugs, buttons, etc., you can always take the DIY route. Zazzle http://creativeyarnentrepreneur.com/Zazzle* is a site that allows you to customize products for small orders and to create your own print-on-demand site for your students.

PUBLIC RELATIONS

If you'd like to get noticed as an expert in your local community or online, I recommend that you sign up for Help A Reporter Out (HARO) https://www.helpareporter.com/ as a source. By responding to requests from journalists, you can establish or build your reputation.

If you're new to the world of public relations, I'd highly recommend *The Little Book of Big PR: 100+ Quick Tips to Get Your Business Noticed* by Jennefer Witter http://creativeyarnentrepreneur.com/littlePR.*

SMALL BUSINESS DEVELOPMENT RESOURCES

In the U.S., there are many free resources available to support small business owners:

- The **Small Business Association (SBA)** operates regional offices https://www.sba.gov/tools/local-assistance/regionaloffices dedicated to helping small business owners succeed.
- The SBA also partners with **Small Business Development Centers** https://www.sba.gov/tools/local-assistance/sbdc throughout the U.S. to provide free counseling and low-cost training.
- **SCORE** https://www.score.org/ is another national organization that provides small business advice for free.
- The **Internal Revenue Service (IRS)** provides online resources and information for small businesses and the self-employed https://www.irs.gov/Businesses/Small-Businesses-&-Self-Employed. You can apply for an Employer Identification Number (EIN) https://www.irs.gov/Businesses/Small-Businesses-&-Self-Employed/Employer-ID-Numbers-EINs online for free. Many business banking accounts require an EIN. You might also prefer to use an EIN rather than your Social Security Number when working as an independent contractor.

Don't forget to look for nearby resources, including those offered by your city, county, or state.

SOCIAL MEDIA

Social media platforms are constantly shifting, so I stay up to date on the marketing implications by following Social Media Examiner http://www.socialmediaexaminer.com/. You can read articles on Social Media Examiner's blog or subscribe to either of its podcasts http://www.socialmediaexaminer.com/podcasts/. The **Social Media Examiner Show** is a 10-minute daily podcast featuring the latest blog articles. **Social Media Marketing with Michael Stelzner** is a 45-minute weekly podcast featuring interviews with social media marketing experts. There are also frequently updated "beginner guides" to the more popular social networks.

You can also learn more about getting started on these social media platforms:

FACEBOOK

- Facebook Pages https://www.facebook.com/business/products/pages
- Facebook Ads https://www.facebook.com/business/products/ads/
- Facebook Groups https://www.facebook.com/help/1628664438847527/
- Facebook Live https://www.facebook.com/help/1636872026560015

INSTAGRAM

- Getting Started https://help.instagram.com/454502981253053/
- Instagram Ads https://www.facebook.com/business/help/976240832426180/

LINKEDIN

- Getting started https://www.linkedin.com/start/join
- Join a group https://www.linkedin.com/help/linkedin/answer/186/finding-and-joining-a-group?lang=en
- Write a long-form post https://www.linkedin.com/help/linkedin/answer/47445/long-form-posts-on-linkedin-overview?lang=en
- Search for class coordinators or education venues https://blog.linkedin.com/2007/07/15/5-tips-on-how-t

PINTEREST

- 🧶 Setting up a business account https://business.pinterest.com/en/set-your-business-account
- 🧶 Promoted Pins (Pinterest ads) https://ads.pinterest.com/

RAVELRY

- 🧶 Getting started http://www.ravelry.com/tour/getting-started
- 🧶 Setting up a designer account to share your original patterns http://www.ravelry.com/tour/designers-welcome
- 🧶 Join or start a group http://www.ravelry.com/wiki/pages/GroupsTab
- 🧶 Ravelry ads http://www.ravelry.com/advertisers

TWITTER

- 🧶 Getting started https://support.twitter.com/articles/215585
- 🧶 Twitter ads https://ads.twitter.com/login

YOUTUBE

- 🧶 Starting a channel https://support.google.com/youtube/answer/1646861?hl=en
- 🧶 Creator Academy https://youtube.com/creatoracademy/page/education?hl=en

TEACHING SITES

These websites specialize in making connections between teachers and students:

- ClassClassifiieds https://www.classclassifieds.com/
- Take Lessons https://takelessons.com/

Sites like these come and go frequently, so be on the lookout for similar sites that are popular in your community.

TREND TRACKING

As a crochet teacher, it's helpful to stay on top of the latest trends in crochet, design, and color. There are many ways to do that, but here are my favorite resources for tracking trends:

- **Ravelry's Hot Right Now** (crochet) search http://www.ravelry.com/patterns/search#view=captioned_thumbs&craft=crochet&sort=recently-popular sorts crochet patterns in order of "hotness," a secret algorithm that measures the current popularity of a pattern. You can also refine the search to include other factors that are more relevant to your target audience, such as free *vs.* premium patterns, project type, gender, or size.

- **Amazon's Best Sellers in Crocheting** http://amzn.to/2456LP7* provides a current sales rank of crochet books. (Unfortunately, it often includes some knitting books, too.) It will usually include a combination of classics and trending topics.

- **Pinterest**'s crochet search https://www.pinterest.com/search/?q=crochet shows popular Pins and is a great way to find projects and patterns that are trending.

- **Pantone** http://www.pantone.com/pages/pantone/index.aspx is a company that developed a standardized "color matching" system to allow different manufacturers in print, design, fabric, and other industries to make matching colors. Pantone releases two free fashion color reports each year (spring and fall), which predict color trends for upcoming seasons. The most recent reports can be found by choosing "Color Intelligence" from the website's menu bar and selecting "Fashion Color Report."

- **BuzzSumo** http://buzzsumo.com/ is a site that allows you to search shareable online content. Type *crochet* into the search bar on the home page and then refine your search to filter by date, language, country, and more. (Note that, occasionally, news stories involving people with the last name Crochet or who are crocheters will outrank crochet-related content.)

Understanding how holidays and other seasonal events impact your classes and marketing efforts is also important. Check this out:

- **Pinterest for Business** has a "Pinterest Planning Calendar" SlideShare presentation http://www.slideshare.net/secret/6TMM1juei1tnB18 with a helpful timeline of seasonal searches.

WEBSITE

As a crochet teacher, you may use your business website as a static business card, have a dynamic blog filled with tutorials, or include e-commerce options for students. Whether you're just starting a website or considering transitioning to a different service, there are so many options available that it can be confusing. Here are some that I've used or heard good things about over the years:

There are numerous options for starting and hosting a free blog or website, but two that I've used are Blogger (e.g., "YourSiteName.blogspot.com") and WordPress.com (e.g., "YourSiteName.wordpress.com"):

- Blogger is part of the Google family and you can find the Getting Started Guide here. https://support.google.com/blogger/answer/1623800?hl=en
- WordPress.com is the fully hosted, free version of WordPress. You can find the Getting Started Guide here. https://wordpress.com/learn-more/?v=site
- Both options allow you to upgrade to a self-hosted option later so that you have a custom domain name (e.g., "YourSiteName.com").

If you would like to customize your domain name, many people (including me) use self-hosted WordPress.org sites:

- To transition to self-hosting, you'll need to pay for a domain name (e.g., "MyCrochetBusiness.com") as well as the services of a web host. I use InMotion Hosting http://creativeyarnentrepreneur.com/InMotion* to host my WordPress sites. Your web host should have Getting Started Guides to help you to set up your own WordPress site.
- If all of this seems overwhelming, Squarespace https://www.squarespace.com/ is an all-in-one solution that includes web hosting, website templates, and tech support with optional e-commerce pages.

WHOLESALE AND DISCOUNTED SUPPLIES

If you sell supplies or class kits to your students, consider opening a wholesale account with a distributer. Two companies I have heard great things about are **Accessories Unlimited** http://www.accessoriesunlimitedinc.com/ and **Darice** https://www.darice.com/. Both have low minimums and a range of supplies.

APPENDICES

This section includes sample forms and templates. You are welcome to copy these forms and templates for use in **your business**, but not to sell or distribute these to others.

MARIE SEGARES
APPENDIX A: CLASS DESCRIPTION TEMPLATE

Class Title: _____

Class Description (internal): _____
_____
_____
_____

Class Description (marketing/ad copy): _____
_____
_____
_____
_____

Date(s): _____ # of Sessions: _____ Cancellation Deadline Date: _____

Start Time: _____ a.m./p.m.   End Time: _____ a.m./p.m.   # of Hours: _____

Location: _____

Travel Directions: _____
_____

Minimum # of Students: _____   Maximum # of Students: _____

Skills Needed To Take This Class: _____
_____
_____

Supplies Students Should Bring To This Class: _____
_____
_____

Required "Homework" Students Should Complete Before Class: _____
_____
_____

Price Per Student: _____   Teaching Course Fee: _____

APPENDIX B: STUDENT LEARNING OBJECTIVES WORKSHEET

Class Title: _____

Session # (for multi-session class): _____

Is there a particular skill or set of skills you want the students to master by the end of class? _____
_____
_____
_____

Is there a project the students should finish by the end of class? _____
_____
_____
_____

If a project can't be finished in class, are there additional skills, tips, or information students will need to learn in class so they can successfully finish the project at home? _____
_____
_____
_____

Learning objective(s) for all students: _____
_____
_____
_____

Learning objective(s) for fast learners: _____
_____
_____

Learning objective(s) for students with previous preparation: _____
_____
_____
_____

APPENDIX C: CLASS OUTLINE TEMPLATE

Class Title: _____ Total # of Hours: ____

Session # (for multi-session class): _____ Length of Session: _____

SESSION AGENDA/SCHEDULE

Start/End Time	Topic
	1)
	2)
	3)
	4)
	5)
	6)
	7)
	8)
	9)
	10)
	11)
	12)
	13)
	14)
	15)

APPENDIX C: CLASS OUTLINE TEMPLATE CONTINUED

Topic #/Description: _____
_____

Expected time for: _____ Teacher Instruction _____ Student Practice

Sample explanation/overview: _____
_____
_____
_____
_____
_____
_____
_____
_____

Materials/tools needed for demonstration: _____
_____
_____
_____
_____

Student practice notes: _____
_____
_____
_____
_____

Student materials/skills required to add to class description: _____
_____
_____
_____

MARIE SEGARES
APPENDIX D: CLASS PACKING LIST TEMPLATE

Course Title: _____

Class Session: _____

- ❑ Class Session Outline
- ❑ Handout Titles: _____
  _____
  _____

  Custom Link (if any): _____
- ❑ Course Evaluations
  # of Copies: _____ or Date Handouts/Evaluations Sent to Class Coordinator: _____
- ❑ Crochet Hook(s) for Demonstration (List Sizes/Types): _____
  _____

- ❑ Yarn for Demonstration (List # of Skeins/Type): _____
  _____

- ❑ Scissors
- ❑ Gauge Check/Ruler/Tailor's Tape
- ❑ Other Notions and Tools for Demonstration (List Types): _____
  _____
  _____

- ❑ Supplies for Student Use in Class (List Types): _____
  _____

- ❑ Swatches or Samples (List Types): _____
  _____

- ❑ Student Sign In Sheet
- ❑ Student Supply Kits (If Applicable, List Items): _____
  _____
  _____

  # of Kits: _____ Price: _____ Pre-Paid/Collect on Site
- ❑ Promotional Items (If Applicable, List Types): _____
  _____

- ❑ Mailing List Sign Up Sheet   ❑ Watch/Alarm Clock
- ❑ Business Cards   ❑ Personal Hygiene Kit
- ❑ Folder   ❑ Water or Water Bottle
- ❑ Notepad/Paper   ❑ Snack
- ❑ Pen/Pencil
- ❑ Other (List Items): _____
  _____

- ❑ Venue ID Card/Keys   Office Code: _____ Copier Code: _____ Restroom Code: _____

APPENDIX E: STUDENT EVALUATION

Class Name: _____

Location: _____

Student Name: _____ Date: _____

Please check your rating for each aspect of the class listed below.

	Strongly Disagree		Neutral		Strongly Agree	
The pace of this class was appropriate.	1	2	3	4	5	Not Applicable
The class was organized.	1	2	3	4	5	Not Applicable
The teacher was effective.	1	2	3	4	5	Not Applicable
I got as much personal attention as I expected to receive in a class of this size.	1	2	3	4	5	Not Applicable
The teacher was easy to understand.	1	2	3	4	5	Not Applicable
I had enough time to practice the techniques and skills the teacher shared.	1	2	3	4	5	Not Applicable
This class was the right length for me.	1	2	3	4	5	Not Applicable
I would recommend this class to a friend.	1	2	3	4	5	Not Applicable
I would recommend this teacher to a friend.	1	2	3	4	5	Not Applicable

What did you like best about the class?

(Turn)

What would you change about the class?

How did you learn about this class?

What type of class or class projects would you like to see in the future?

What types of projects are you interested in making?

Other Comments:

How would you rate your own crochet skills?
- ❏ Beginner
- ❏ Advanced Beginner
- ❏ Intermediate
- ❏ Expert

Check here ___ to allow the teacher to use your comments for marketing purposes (e.g., on website, in brochures).

Check here ___ to allow the teacher to use your full name with these comments. Otherwise, initials will be used.

To subscribe to the teacher's email list, write your email address here:

_____

IF YOU ENJOYED THIS BOOK

If you enjoyed this book and it has helped your crochet business, I'd really appreciate it if you would do one (or all three) of these things for me.

WRITE A REVIEW

Reviews help me find new readers. Write whatever you'd like, but if you're having trouble getting started, share:

- What you enjoyed about the book
- What you didn't like about the book
- Three things from the book that you plan to change or start in your business
- Any results you have already seen from changes you made based on the book

Go to http://creativeyarnentrepreneur.com/mmtcreview to share your review. After you write the review, I'd love to know more about it! You can email me at marie@creativeyarnentrepreneur.com to let me know so I can thank you. Don't forget to tell me a bit about yourself so I can get to know you.

SUBSCRIBE TO THE CREATIVE YARN ENTREPRENEUR EMAIL LIST

You can find out about upcoming books, events, and the latest podcast episodes through my email newsletter. Visit http://creativeyarnentrepreneur.com/mmtclist to sign up.

SUBSCRIBE TO THE CREATIVE YARN ENTREPRENEUR SHOW PODCAST

The Creative Yarn Entrepreneur Show is a biweekly podcast where can find great ideas for launching, managing, and evolving your yarn-related business along with tips for keeping yourself product, creative, and sane. To subscribe to the Show on your favorite app, visit http://creativeyarnentrepreneur.com/subscribe.

Thanks for your support!

ABOUT THE AUTHOR

Marie Segares is a crochet and knitting designer, teacher, blogger, and podcaster. Marie has been sharing crochet and knitting patterns, tips, reviews, and her crafty adventures on the Underground Crafter blog since 2011. In 2014, she launched the Creative Yarn Entrepreneur Show, a biweekly podcast for yarn-industry indies.

Marie's patterns, articles, and tutorials have been published in *Crochetvolution*, *Crochet World*, *Entwine*, *I Like Crochet*, *I Like Knitting*, *Inside Crochet*, *KnitCircus*, *Love of Crochet*, *Love of Knitting*, *Pom Pom Quarterly*, and the *Quick & Simple Crochet* booklet series.

In addition to private lessons, Marie has taught crochet or knitting classes through Barnard College Student Life, Adult School of Montclair, Brooklyn Workshop Gallery, DC37 Saturday Activities, Michaels, Mount Vernon Hotel Museum, and Queens Public Library. She has also taught at regional fiber festivals including the Finger Lakes Fiber Arts Festival, the North Jersey Fiber Arts Festival, and the Pittsburgh Knit and Crochet Festival.

Marie is a professional member of, and volunteer blogger for, the Crochet Guild of America. She is a designer/teacher member of The Knitting Guild Association and an affiliate member of The National NeedleArts Association.

Marie is a graduate of Barnard College and earned master's degrees from Columbia University Mailman School of Public Health and New York University Stern School of Business. She lives in New York City.

www.ingramcontent.com/pod-product-compliance
Lightning Source LLC
Chambersburg PA
CBHW080551170426
43195CB00016B/2755